Workbook to Accompany

Music

IN THEORY AND PRACTICE

Volume II

Sixth Edition

Bruce Benward
University of Wisconsin-Madison

Gary White
Iowa State University

Boston, Massachusetts   Burr Ridge, Illinois   Dubuque, Iowa
Madison, Wisconsin   New York, New York   San Francisco, California   St. Louis, Missouri

The McGraw-Hill Companies Higher Education Group
A Division of The McGraw-Hill Companies

Workbook to accompany
Benward/White, Music in Theory and Practice, Volume II, Sixth Edition

2 3 4 5 6 7 8 9 0 QPD QPD 9 0 9 8

ISBN 0-697-32876-7

CONTENTS

PREFACE

The workbook anthologies to accompany *Music in Theory and Practice,* volumes 1 and 2, provide assignments to augment those printed in the texts. They also include anthologies of music for study. The chapters of the workbooks bear the same titles as those of the texts and are correlated to them. The pieces in the anthology sections are referred to in the assignments, but the instructor is encouraged to use these pieces in any way he or she feels appropriate.

The workbooks contain three different types of assignments:

1. *Drill.* This type of assignment acquaints students with the basic material in the corresponding chapter in the text. In general, the topics are isolated from surrounding musical context to permit a grasp of the more obvious and elementary aspects. Learning to spell chords in various keys, distinguishing between chords in isolation, and identifying musical designs in artificially prepared situations are examples of drill exercises.
2. *Analysis.* This type of assignment acquaints students with music literature, permits them to view chapter material in its actual settings, and allows them to observe conformity as well as digression from the norm. If done diligently, these exercises will also noticeably improve sight-reading ability and dexterity in analysis.
3. *Composition.* After completing the extensive drill and comprehensive analysis assignments provided by these workbooks, students are encouraged to try their own hands at employing musical ideas, chord progressions, phrase relationships, and so on, in the context of a musical composition. This comprises the ultimate test of a student's comprehension. If the devices that were drilled and analyzed can be successfully manipulated in a composition, one of the most important goals in the study of music theory has been achieved.

The workbook/anthologies include guided review and self-testing sections. Each chapter contains a suggested strategy for reviewing and learning the material. Students often find that the study skills they have developed for other courses don't work well in learning music theory. The guided review sections present a step-by-step process involving reading, playing musical examples, and writing, which will establish good study habits and help ensure success in learning the material.

Each chapter concludes with a review and a "self test" covering the essential concepts of the chapter. Answers for all chapter tests are contained in a section beginning on page 219. These tests allow the student to identify areas of strength and weakness before, rather than during, examinations.

BRUCE BENWARD
GARY WHITE

I LATE RENAISSANCE POLYPHONY

Name _____

Section _____

Date _____

A. Refer to Lassus's *Sicut rosa* on page 178. Provide a complete analysis of *Sicut rosa* using the analysis of *Beatus homo* (chapter 1, volume 2, of the textbook) as a model.
1. Indicate the intervals between the two voices throughout.
2. Circle all dissonant intervals and identify:
    a.   *Unaccented passing tone*
    b.   *Accented passing tone*
    c.   *Suspension*
    d.   *Portamento*
    e.   *Nota cambiata*
3. Indicate all imitation by marking with a highlighter or in any other appropriate manner.
4. Name also:
    a. The mode of the composition
    b. The accidentals and the reason for their use
    c. The cadence points and the types of cadences used
    d. The text painting in evidence
    e. The treatment of the text—whether syllabic or melismatic

Text	Translation
Sicut rosa,	Just as a rose,
sicut rosa inter spinas illas audit speciem,	Just as a rose among thorns lends its beauty even to them,
sic renustat suam Virgo Maria progeniem, Maria progeniem,	In the same way the Virgin Mary imparts her grace and charm over all her subjects,
germinavit enim florem,	From her has sprung a flower,
qui vitalem dat odorem, qui vitalem dat odorem.	Whose aroma is the gift of life.

B. Apply the same analytical techniques described in section A to Lassus's *Sancti mei.* (Refer to page 177.)

Text	Translation
Sancti mei, sancti mei,	My divine people, my divine people
qui in isto saeculo certamen habuistis,	Who in this world have known only hard labor and conflict,
mercedem laborum vestrorum ego reddam vobis,	I shall give to you satisfaction for your endeavors,
ego reddam vobis,	For your endeavors,
ego reddam vobis.	For your endeavors.

C. The following short excerpt contains a number of stylistic errors—musical devices that were foreign to the strict sacred vocal style of the sixteenth century.
1. Find each error and place a number on the score at the point of the error.
2. In the blanks below the score, indicate the nature of the error.
3. The first error is recorded correctly in the example (Ex. 1).

Composition containing errors:

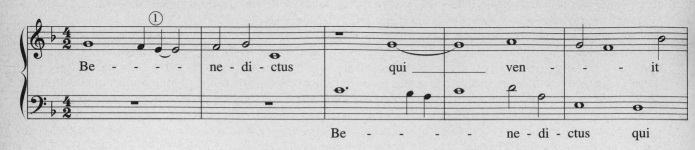

Errors:

(Ex.) 1. <u>A note should not be tied to a succeeding note of longer value.</u>

2. _____

3. _____

4. _____

5. _____

6. _____

7. _____

8. _____

9. _____

10. _____

11. _____

12. _____

D. Refer to the *Benedictus* from *Missa pro defunctis* by Lassus on page 176. Apply the same analytical techniques described in section A to this composition in three parts.

REVIEW

1. Review the consonant and dissonant intervals on page 6 of the textbook. Every dissonant interval should be circled in your analysis and explained as one of the dissonance types listed on pages 7–11.

2. Review the dissonance types on pages 7–11. Study the musical examples illustrating each device, and play them over to hear the musical effect of the dissonance (singing them with a friend is even better). Pay particular attention to the decorations of suspensions, which may confuse you when you see them in a work you are analyzing. The *nota cambiata* also deserves special consideration because it is unique to the sixteenth-century style and you will not have seen it before.

3. Study the section on melody on pages 11–12, paying particular attention to the treatment of skips in a melody. Stepwise motion in the opposite direction preceding and following a skip has the effect of "smoothing out" the skip and thus diminishing its impact on the flow of the melody. Note the intervals that are avoided: ascending M6ths, descending 6ths, 7ths, diminished and augmented intervals, and skips greater than an octave. What intervals are allowed as skips?

4. Examine the list of common note values and note values that do not occur on pages 12–14. The subject of rhythm in sixteenth-century counterpoint is very complex, and the summary presented here is far from exhaustive. Look at individual voices of one of the works cited in the textbook and observe the rhythmic material in relation to the summary in the textbook.

5. Find several examples of *clausula vera* in the works cited in the textbook. Can you find a *clausula vera* that is not preceded by a suspension?

6. Listen to examples of sixteenth-century music (Palestrina, Lassus, Victoria, and others) to gain a sense of the style. Careful listening and performing the music are necessary to gain an appreciation of the style.

TEST YOURSELF I

Answers are on page 219.

1. Analyze the excerpt from *Justus cor suum tradet* quoted below by labeling each interval between the voices.
2. Circle all dissonances and label each one. Use figure 1.31 on page 18 of the textbook as a model for this chapter.
3. Label the beginning of each point of imitation by drawing a line between the first note of each line.
4. In measure 6, a **B**♭ appears in the lower voice. Why is this **B**♭ necessary?
5. Examine all the note values in each line. Do you observe any deviations from the principles stated on pp. 12–14?
6. A *clausula vera* occurs in measure_____.
7. The mode of this composition is_____.

Lassus: *Justus cor suum tradet.*

A. Have a piano major play Invention no. 1 in C Major by Bach (page 127). Arrange it for two instruments or *swingle sing* it in class (sing the tones on a syllable such as *la, lu,* or *ta*).
   1. Do a roman numeral analysis and/or macro analysis of this invention.
   2. Above and below the score indicate the following:
      a. Each statement of the *motive* and *countermotive*
      b. All segments of the sequences
      c. Free material
      d. Motive-derived or countermotive-derived material
      e. The various sections of the two-part invention
      f. The types of cadences that punctuate the composition
   3. Discuss in class:
      a. The similarities and differences between this invention and the one analyzed in chapter 2 of the textbook, "Two-Voice, Eighteenth-Century Counterpoint"
      b. The handling of dissonance

B. Write a two-part invention in eighteenth-century-style counterpoint.
   1. Pattern the form of your invention after no. 1 of Bach's inventions.
   2. Write the composition for any instrument or instruments that can be played in class.
   3. Make up a *motive* of your own or use one of the following.

1. D Major

2. E Major

3. B♭ Major

4. C Minor

4. Perform the composition in class. Then, using an opaque or overhead projector, have the class *swingle sing* each student's composition.

REVIEW

1. Review the description of a typical two-part invention on pages 29–31 of the textbook. Pay particular attention to the musical examples and how the various motives and sequences are labeled. Study figure 2.4 in detail.
2. Study the section on writing two-voice counterpoint on pages 36–38. Review in particular the section on avoiding parallel perfect intervals. The restrictions on parallel perfect intervals are more stringent in two-part writing than in four-part chorale styles.
3. Listen to a recording of the two-part inventions or play several at a keyboard. Careful listening is an important adjunct to study of the text.

TEST YOURSELF 2

Answers are on page 220.

1. Examine the following two-part invention and listen to a recording or play it.
2. Measure 1 contains a statement of the_____.
3. The lower part in measure 2 is the_____in imitation. The interval of imitation is a(n)_____. The right-hand part in measure 2 is the_____.
4. Measures 4–6 are a good example of a_____.
5. The second part of the invention begins in measure_____. It is in the_____key (relation to the tonic).
6. In measure 27 in the right hand there is a statement of the_____in the_____key.
7. Provide a roman numeral analysis of this invention. Refer to figure 2.4 in the textbook as a model.
8. Invention number 10 is in_____sections.

Bach: Invention no. 10, BWV 781, in G Major, from Fifteen Two-Part Inventions.

3 THE FUGUE

Name _____

Section _____

Date _____

A. Refer to Bach's Fugue no. 6 in D Minor from the *Well-Tempered Clavier*, book 1, on page 122. Have a piano major play this three-voice fugue. Arrange it for three instruments or *swingle sing* it in class.
1. Do a roman numeral analysis and/or macro analysis of this fugue.
2. Use a highlighter or any other appropriate way to indicate or label the following:
    a. Each statement of the *subject, answer,* and *countersubject*
    b. The type of answer—whether *tonal* or *real*
    c. All segments of sequences
    d. The larger sections of the composition: the *exposition* and all *episodes* and *entries*
    e. The various keys represented in the composition
    f. The cadence points and the types of cadences used
    g. Any *bridges, codettas,* or *links*

B. Using the same approach as in section A of this chapter, provide a complete analysis of Bach's Fugue no. 7 in E-Flat Major from the *Well-Tempered Clavier* book 1, on page 124. Compare the form and general makeup of this fugue with that of the Fugue no. 6 in D Minor (section A of this chapter).

C. Write the *exposition* of a three-voice fugue in eighteenth-century-style counterpoint.
1. Pattern the form of the exposition after the Bach Fugue in C Minor, in chapter 3 of the textbook.
2. Write the exposition for any instrument or instrumental combination that can assure a performance in class.
3. Use one of the fugue subjects in the following list.
4. Perform the compositions in class. Then, using an opaque or overhead projector, have the class *swingle sing* each student's composition.

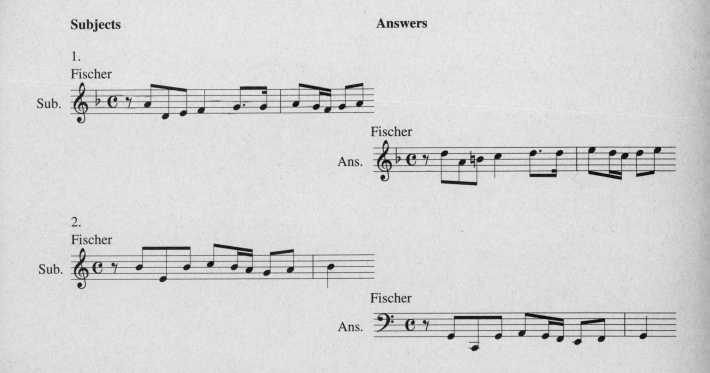

D. Add episodes and entries to the fugue exposition written in section C. Continue to pattern the fugue after the Bach Fugue in C Minor. Then write a concluding statement that returns to the original key.

REVIEW

1. Look at the list of terms at the head of the chapter (page 47) and provide a definition for each term. Check your definition with that given in the chapter. There are more terms associated with the fugue than many other forms, and you will need a command of the terminology to analyze or discuss its contents.
2. Study figure 3.10 in the textbook after listening to the fugue. There is a great deal of information about the structure of fugues in the labels on this work. The summary chart on pages 59–60 will give you an overall picture of the form of this work.
3. Listen to other fugues by Bach and see if you can analyze them using the terminology of this chapter. The forty-eight fugues of the *Well-Tempered Clavier* will provide ample works for study.

TEST YOURSELF 3

Answers are on page 221.

Questions 1–3 refer to the following three excerpts from Bach fugues.

1. Bach: Fugue in G Major, BWV 561.

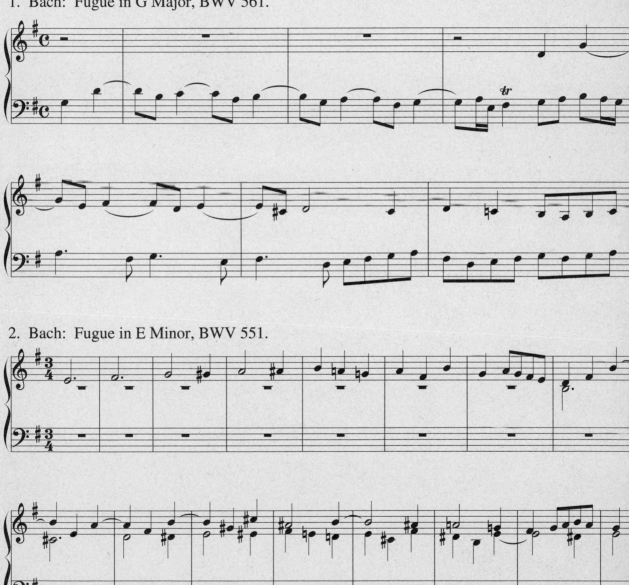

2. Bach: Fugue in E Minor, BWV 551.

3. Bach: Fugue in C Minor, BWV 574.

1. In example 1 (Fugue in G Major, BWV 561) the subject is given a (real/tonal) answer (circle one). If it is tonal, explain the modification(s) and state the reason for a tonal answer.
2. In example 2 (Fugue in E Minor, BWV 551) the subject is given a (real/tonal) answer (circle one). If it is tonal, explain the modification(s) and state the reason for a tonal answer.
3. In example 3 (Fugue in C Minor, BWV 574) the subject is given a (real/tonal) answer (circle one). If it is tonal, explain the modification(s) and state the reason for a tonal answer.
4. Analyze the following short fugue of Bach using figure 3.10 (pages 55–59 in the textbook) as a model.

Bach: Fugue in D Minor, BWV 899.

4 BORROWED CHORDS

Name _____

Section _____

Date _____

A. The following are four-part chorale phrases.
1. Add alto and tenor according to the figured-bass symbols.
2. Provide a complete harmonic analysis.

1.

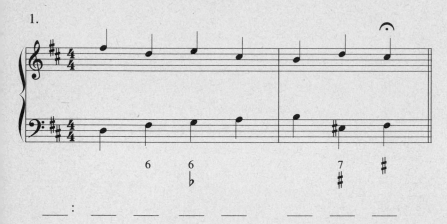

___ : ___ ___ ___ ___ ___ ___ ___

2.

___ : ___ ___ ___ ___ ___ ___ ___

3.

___ : ___ ___ ___ ___ ___ ___ ___

4.

5.

6.

7.

Chromatic Harmony

B. Add accidentals to this composition to create borrowed chords. Remember that too many borrowed chords will simply revert the entire composition to the parallel minor mode.

C. Write a short composition of sixteen measures.

1. Use the following form:

Phrase	Phrase Relationship	Key	Cadence
1	A	B♭ Major	Half
2	B (Contrasting)	B♭ Major	Authentic
3	A'	B♭ Major	Half
4	B' (Contrasting)	B♭ Major	Authentic

2. Use the following chord progressions:

Phrase 1

I ii°⁶ vii°⁷/V I⁶₄ V

Phrase 2

I VI ii°⁶ V I

Phrase 3

I iv vii°⁷/V I⁶₄ V

Phrase 4

I vii°⁷ I V⁷ I

3. Use homophonic texture (melody with chordal accompaniment).
4. Write for any instrument, instruments, or voice as long as the compositions can be performed by class members.
5. Play the composition in class.
6. After it is played as written, replay the composition making all borrowed chords diatonic (remove accidentals). Have the students determine whether they prefer the diatonic chords or the borrowed chords.

D. Following are eight phrases containing only a figured bass. These are similar in type to the chorale phrases in section A, page 15, except that the soprano melody is not provided.
1. Copy the figured bass on a separate sheet of score paper and include a blank staff line above and below it.
2. On a separate staff, write out the notes of the chords in simple position, in accordance with the figured-bass symbols. For phrase 1, your score should look like this:

3. Fashion a suitable soprano melody to accompany the bass melody. If you are not quite sure what a suitable melody is, examine several chorale melodies. Some suggestions follow:
    a. For the time being, use note-for-note values (in this case, quarter notes). Of course, chorale melodies are not made up entirely of quarter notes, but unless you have already had considerable experience, it is better to write conservatively.
    b. Downward (pitch) motion is used more often than upward when approaching a cadence and when the bass voice ascends. Contrary motion between bass and soprano is usually preferred over similar motion and much preferred over parallel motion.
    c. Try at least two or three different soprano melodies before you make a final decision. Choose the one you think is most compatible with the bass line.
    d. As you are writing the soprano melodies, continually check the chords to make sure that the melody notes you have chosen are indeed chord tones. For the moment, each soprano melody note should be consonant with the bass note that sounds with it.
4. When a suitable soprano melody has been achieved, begin to add the alto and tenor voices. When completed, check again to make sure that all four voices are compatible and that no errors have mysteriously appeared.
5.   Occasionally, the chosen soprano melody may force you to make the voice leading of the alto and tenor voices impossible or, at best, awkward and unmusical. If that unfortunate occurrence should develop, a reworking of the soprano melody is your only choice.
6. Make a harmonic analysis of each completed four-voice phrase.

Chromatic Harmony

REVIEW

1. Study figure 4.1 on page 69 of the textbook, particularly the second line, where the most common borrowed chords in major keys are listed. Choose a major key and spell these five borrowed chords. Continue until you can easily spell all of the chords.

2. Study figure 4.7 (page 74 of the textbook), which illustrates the most common progressions from each of the borrowed chords in major. Notice that all of the borrowed chords are commonly followed by the dominant chord except the **vii°7**, which is followed by the tonic chord. Choose a major key and practice writing each of the borrowed chords in four parts and resolving it to the dominant chord or tonic as appropriate. Continue practicing in various keys until you can easily resolve any of the common borrowed chords in major.

3. Play each of the progressions you have written in number 2 above to familiarize yourself with the musical effect of the borrowed chords.

TEST YOURSELF 4

Answers are on page 223.

The following are examples of the five most common borrowed chords, from minor keys to major keys.

1. Analyze the borrowed chord. Analysis can be effected by determining the chord type (**ii°** is a diminished triad, **ii°7** is a diminished-diminished 7th chord, **iv** is a minor triad, **VI** is a major triad, and **vii°7** is a diminished minor 7th chord).

2. Name the key in which the example functions as a *borrowed* chord.

3. Write the chord that normally follows the given chord in four-part harmony.

4. Provide a roman numeral analysis for both chords.

NEAPOLITAN 6TH CHORDS

. Complete the following voice-leading exercises. Note that some of the later phrases contain a modulation.
1. Add tenor and alto to the figured-bass chorale phrases.
2. Provide an analysis of each chord.

4.

5.

6.

7.

8.

9.

10.

11.

B. Following are eight phrases containing only a figured bass. These are similar in type to the assignment in chapter 4, section D, page 18.
1. Compose an appropriate soprano melody for each of the phrases.
2. Fill in the alto and tenor voices.
3. Make a complete harmonic analysis of each phrase.

Chromatic Harmony

Name _____

Section _____

Date _____

C. Following are three chorale melodies.
1. List the three possible triads that can be used to support each quarter note.
2. Harmonize the melody on scratch paper using only root-position diatonic triads in block style.
3. Substitute secondary dominants, Neapolitan 6th chords, and other altered chords for some of the triads.
4. Sketch in a bass line that has sufficient contrary motion to the melody and contains an appropriate contour.
5. Add the remaining voices using recommended part-writing procedures.
6. Add nonharmonic tones where appropriate.
7. Make a complete harmonic analysis of your composition.

1.

2.

3.

D. The following (example a) is a short, four-voice composition.
    1. Making this the basis for another composition:
        a.   Complete the composition (at b).
        b.   Continue the figure as shown in the first two measures.
        c.   Place the figure in any voice.
        d.   Use one chord per measure throughout.
        e.   Expand the final chord into two measures.
        f.   Make a complete harmonic analysis.
        g.   Add tempo markings.
        h.   Add all necessary marks for interpretation.

a.

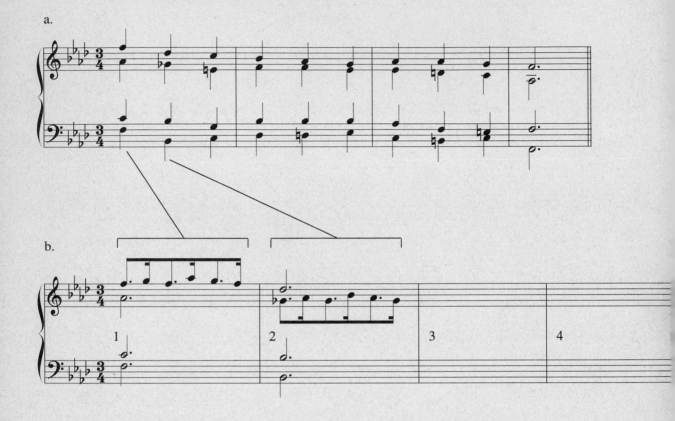

b.

Chromatic Harmony

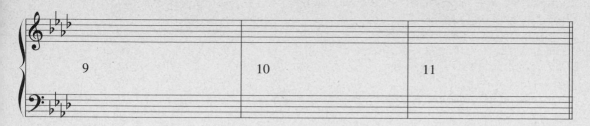

E. The following are excerpts from songs by Schubert and Haydn. Provide a complete harmonic analysis.

Schubert: *Der Müller und der Bach* (The Miller and the Brook) from *Die Schöne Müllerin*
(The Miller's Beautiful Daughter), op. 25, no. 19, D. 795.

Haydn: *Lob der Faulheit* (Praise of Idleness), Hob. XXVIa:22.

Chromatic Harmony

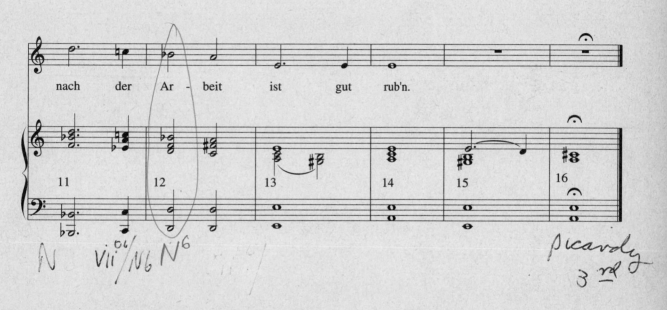

REVIEW

1. Select a major triad and name the keys in which it would be the Neapolitan 6th chord (both major and minor). Continue practicing until you can quickly name the key.
2. Turn to the circle of fifths (figure 2.17 on page 38 of volume 1). For each key spell the Neapolitan 6th chord.
3. Study figure 5.9 on page 84 of the textbook, which illustrates proper voice leading for the Neapolitan 6th chord. Practice writing and resolving the **N⁶** chord in a variety of major and minor keys, using figure 5.11 as a guide. Pay particular attention to example **e**, which shows the way to avoid parallel 5ths in resolving the Neapolitan 6th to the tonic six-four.

Answers are on page 223.

A. Each given triad in four-part harmony is the **V** chord in a minor key.

1. Determine the key (minor), and write it in the appropriate place.
2. Determine the Neapolitan 6th chord in this key, and write it in four-part harmony so that it leads smoothly to the **V** triad.
3. Place the analysis beneath each chord (see measure 1 for an example).

1. (Ex.)   2.   3.   4.

am: N 6   V   B♭♯ m   F♯ ♯ m   E♯ ♯ m   V

B. Complete in the same manner as A. The **vii°⁷/V** is added between the **N⁶** and the **V** triad (see measure 5 for an example).

5. (Ex.)   6.   7.   8.

fm: N 6   vii°⁷/V   V

C. Complete in the same manner as A. The **i$^6_4$** chord is added between the **N⁶** and the **V** triad (see measure 9 for an example).

9. (Ex.)   10.   11.   12.

cm: N 6   i$^6_4$ V

6 AUGMENTED 6TH CHORDS

Name _____

Section _____

Date _____

A. Write an Italian augmented 6th chord above each given tone. Use the most conventional position of the chord. The given tone is the lowest note of the chord.

1. (Ex.)   2.   3.   4.   5.   6.   7.   8.   9.   10.

B. Write an German augmented 6th chord above each given tone. Use the most conventional position of the chord.

1. (Ex.)   2.   3.   4.   5.   6.   7.   8.   9.   10.

C. Write an French augmented 6th chord above each given tone. Use the most conventional position of the chord.

1. (Ex.)   2.   3.   4.   5.   6.   7.   8.   9.   10.

D. Complete the following exercises in the following manner:
1. Add tenor and alto to the figured-bass chorale phrases.
2. Make an analysis of each chord.

1.

2.

31

3.

4.

5.

6.

7.

8.

9.

10.

Augmented 6th Chords   33

E. The following eight phrases contain only a figured bass. These are similar in type to the assignments in chapter 4, section D, page 18, and chapter 5, page 24.
1. Compose an appropriate soprano melody for each of the phrases.
2. Fill in the alto and tenor voices.
3. Make a complete harmonic analysis of each phrase.

Chromatic Harmony

Name _____

Section _____

Date _____

F. The four short excerpts shown here contain augmented 6th chords. Provide a complete harmonic analysis of each. Excerpt 1 illustrates conventional treatment.

1. Beethoven: Bagatelle in G Minor, op. 119, no. 1.

Excerpt 2 contains one example in which an augmented 6th chord includes a nonharmonic upper pedal tune.

2. Schubert: Sonata in A Minor, op. 42, D. 845.

Augmented 6th Chords

35

Can you account for the spelling of the augmented 6th chord in excerpt 3?

3. Schumann: *Drei Stücklein* (Three Pieces) from *Bunte Blätter* (Multicolored Leaves), op. 99, no. 3.

In excerpt 4, augmented 6th chords are given traditional treatment, but measures 5 through 7 contain some curious modal mixtures.

4. Schubert: *Die Liebe hat gelogen* (The Love Has Lied), op. 23, no. 1, D. 751.

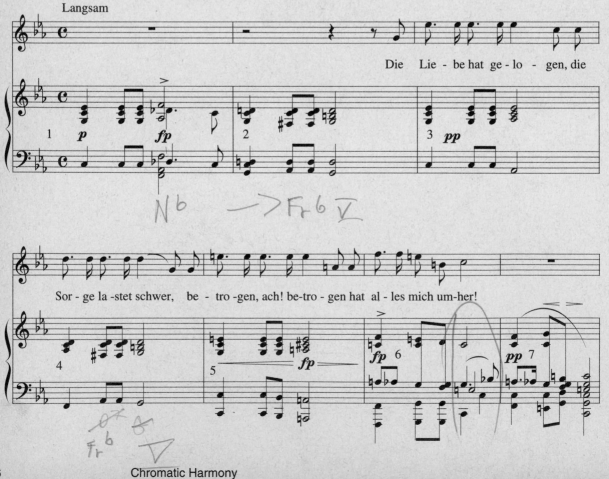

G. Analyze the following excerpt from a Mozart string quartet.
1. Provide a complete harmonic analysis.
2. Is the augmented 6th chord employed conventionally?
3. How does the spacing of instruments in this composition compare with that of the baroque four-part chorales?
4. Review the range of each of the instruments used in a string quartet.

Mozart: String Quartet in A Major, K. 464, I.

1. Study figure 6.2 on page 93 of the textbook, which shows the three common notes among the augmented 6th chords. Practice writing the common notes above various notes, and then add the extra tones to create the **Gr⁶** and **Fr⁶** in each case. Identify the major or minor key where you would likely find each chord.
2. Turn to the circle of fifths (figure 2.17 on page 38 of volume 1) and spell the three augmented 6th chords in each key. Write each chord in four-part harmony, and resolve the augmented 6th in the most conventional way (outward to an octave). Fill in the remaining voices to spell the dominant chord (or the tonic six-four in the case of the **Gr⁶**). Study figure 6.14 on page 99 of the text for proper voice-leading procedures.
3. The **Gr⁶** chord is spelled enharmonically in major keys (study figure 6.14 c and d). Check your work in number 2 above to make sure that the **Gr⁶** chord is correctly spelled in major keys. If not, change the spelling to avoid chromatic resolution of the 5th above the bass in the **Gr⁶** chord.

Test Yourself 6
Answers are on page 224.

Each of the following chords is an augmented 6th chord in four-part harmony. Identify and label the augmented 6th chord (**It⁶**, **Gr⁶**, or **Fr⁶**). Identify the key in which the particular augmented 6th chord is most often found. Write a chord that represents the most conventional resolution of the given chord in four parts, using proper voice leading. Analyze the resolution chord.

VARIATION TECHNIQUE

Name _____

Section _____

Date _____

A. Have a pianist play each of the following excerpts in class.
1. Make a complete harmonic analysis.
2. On the scores themselves, circle nonharmonic tones and name the type (abbreviate or use initials).
3. Discuss:
    a. The variation techniques used by each composer. Indicate whether each variation is essentially melodic, harmonic, rhythmic, contrapuntal, etc., or a combination of techniques.
    b. The type of variation form—*continuous variation* or *theme and variation.*
    c. The relationship of each variation to the original theme.
4. Arrange some of the excerpts for instruments played by class members and perform them.

Brahms: *Chaconne* after J. S. Bach (BWV 1016) from Five Studies for the Piano.

The Classical Period (1750–1825)

Bach: "Goldberg" Variations (Aria with Thirty Variations), BWV 988.

Variation no. 1

Variation no. 3

Variation no. 7

Change in meter, embell melody, rhythm motive

Variation no. 10

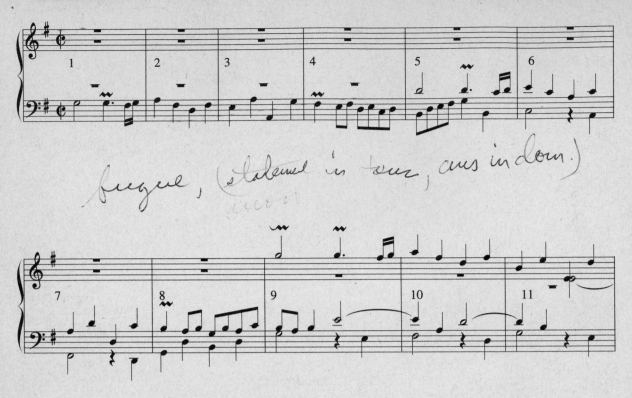

fugue, (elaborert in tow, aus in dom.)
mon

Variation no. 18

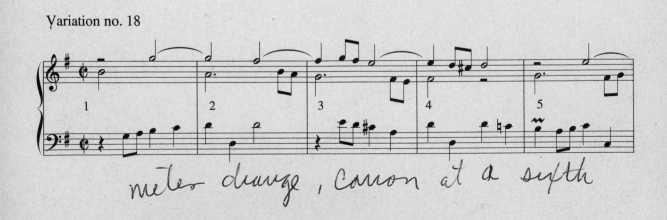

meter change, canon at a sixth

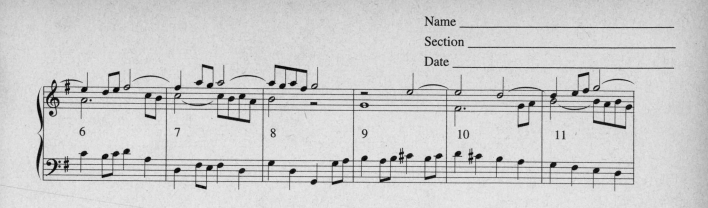

Buxtehude: Ciacona in C Minor, BuxWV 159.

Variation Technique

The Classical Period (1750–1825)

Name _____

Section _____

Date _____

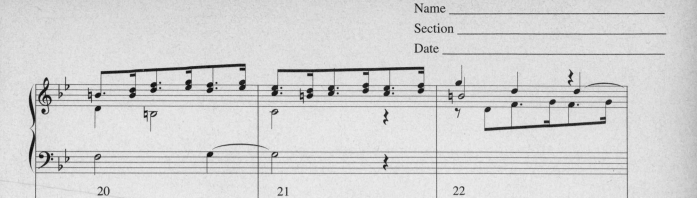

Beethoven: Thirty-two Variations on an Original Theme in C Minor for Piano, WoO 80.

Variation no. 1

Variation no. 7

Variation no. 9

Variation no. 12

Variation no. 18

Variation no. 22

Variation no. 30

Schumann: Theme with Variations from *Drei Clavier-Sonaten für die Jugend* (Three Piano Sonatas for the Young), op. 118.

zurückhaltend　　　*Im Takt.*

Etwas langsamer

REVIEW

1. This chapter presents two types of variations:
   a. continuous variations
   b. theme and variations

   Read the short sections on pages 109 and 110 that describe each type. Make sure that you understand the differences between them.
2. Study the variation techniques discussed on pages 111–115 , paying particular attention to the musical examples. For your convenience, the techniques are listed on page 115 of the textbook.
3. Theme and variation movements abound in the classical and romantic periods. Listen to a number of such movements, and try to identify instances of each of the variation techniques.

TEST YOURSELF 7

Answers are on page 224.

The following questions refer to excerpts from Mozart's variations on the familiar tune "Twinkle, Twinkle Little Star" (Variations on *Ah vous dirais-je, Maman,* K. 265). The first section of the theme is stated below:

Mozart: Variations on *Ah vous dirais-je, Maman*   (Ah, Shall I Tell You, Mama), K. 265.

1. Theme

1. For each of the following excerpts, identify the theme by circling the notes of the original melody.
2. Identify the variation technique(s) employed in each variation, referring to the list of variation techniques on page 115 of the textbook. Some variations contain more than one technique.

2. Variation I

Variation techniques:

3. Variation II

Variation techniques: *Change in harmony, alberti bass*

4. Variation V

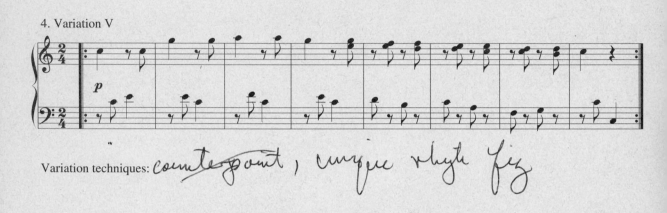

Variation techniques: *counterpoint, unique rhythm fig*

5. Variation VII

change in voice, harmony

embell, extended range

Variation techniques:

6. Variation VIII

Variation techniques: *counterpoint, mode change*

7. Variation XI

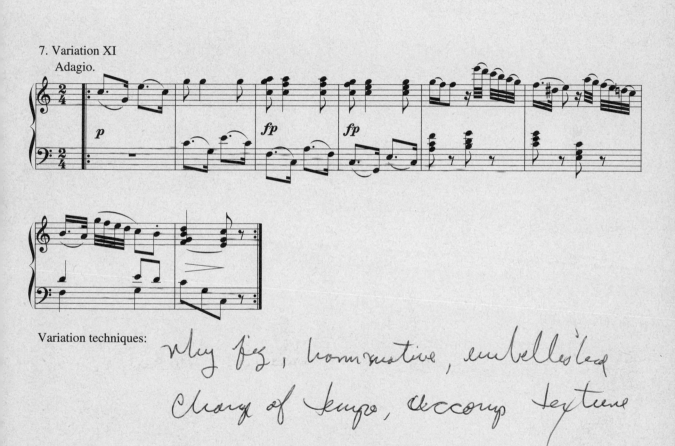

Variation techniques: *rhy fig, harm motive, embellished change of tempo, accomp texture*

8. Variation XII

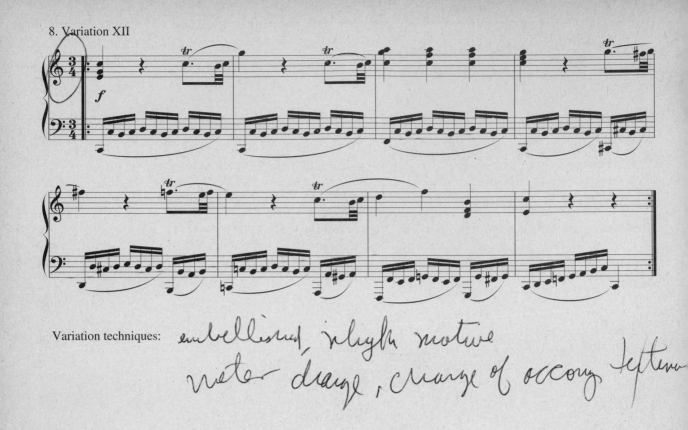

Variation techniques: embellished, rhythm motive
meter change, change of occomp textures

Name _____

Section _____

Date _____

A.   Refer to page 180 to make a complete analysis of Mozart's Piano Sonata, K. 283 (I). Use as a model the analysis found in chapter 8 of the textbook. The form of this sonata allegro movement is fairly traditional, but the following suggestions will assist in understanding some slight departures.

1.   While the material in most development sections can be traced easily to first theme, second theme, transitions, etc., deriving the source of material in this development is somewhat more diffcult. The development, quite short by most standards, begins with carefully camouflaged characteristics of theme 1 (first theme of the exposition).

2.   This movement contains some excellent examples of linear progressions. The normal stream of circle progressions is occasionally interrupted for what may be described as melodic (or linear) priorities. The following excerpt from this movement is an excellent example. Note how the harmony moves in parallel lockstep with the melody and ceases to create definite chord progressions. In measure 47, strong harmonic progressions (**ii V^7 I**) are temporarily restored but then lapse again into linear movement (measure 48).

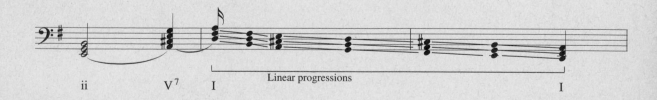

3. Other examples of linear progressions occur in measures 16–21, 83–88, 111–113, and 115–116.
4. Measures 34, 39, 101, and 106 contain harmony that changes every eighth note. While analyzing each chord may provide good practice, other approaches might explain the nature of these measures more precisely.

B. Refer to Haydn's Sonata in G Major (I) on page 168 . Use as a model the analysis found in chapter 8 of the textbook. Some problems are as follows:
1. *Possible overlapping phrases.* Melodically, some phrases are constructed to lead directly to the next without pause. An example is at measures 35–36. One interpretation, based on harmonic influence (**V** to **I**), would consider the first beat of measure 36 as an overlap—both the end of the concluding phrase and the beginning of the next. Another interpretation, based strictly on the melodic content, would consider that the concluding phrase ends on the last beat of measure 35, and the new one begins on the first beat of measure 36—thus no overlap. Both interpretations have merit.
2. *Determining phrase lengths.* In this movement, the frequent lack of a melodic hiatus creates difficulty in determining the length of phrases. For example, are measures 12 (upbeat)–24 comprised of one or two phrases? Melodic content might suggest two (measures 12–16 and 16–24), whereas the lack of a melodic hiatus and absence of a strong cadence would imply only one.
3. *Content of the development section.* Although the restless nature of the development is preserved in this section, the origin of the melodic content may prove more difficult to determine.
4. *Content of the recapitulation.* Do not assume that the recapitulation is simply a rewrite (in the tonic key) of the exposition.

C. Following the same procedures outlined in chapter 8 of the textbook, analyze Beethoven's Piano Sonata in G Major, op. 14, no. 2 (I) on page 132.

REVIEW

1. Study the brief outline of a standard sonata form on p. 125 of the textbook.
2. Study the description of the sections of a sonata form on page 139–142. For each section compare the description to the corresponding section in the Mozart sonata movement analyzed in figure 8.2. You can use this analysis as a model for your own analysis of sonata movements.
3. The first movement of most classical period sonatas, string quartets, and symphonies is in sonata form. Listen to a number of such works, and try to identify the following factors:

I. Exposition
   a. First theme
   b. Transition
   c. Second theme
   d. Third (closing) theme
   e. Codetta
II. Development
   a. Appearance of themes 1 and 2
   b. Retransition
III. Recapitulation
   a. First theme
   b. Transition
   c. Second theme
   d. Third (closing) theme
   e. Coda

You may not find all the elements listed in the outline, and some movements may contain additional elements such as introductions and new themes in the development.

TEST YOURSELF 8

Answers are on page 227.

The following questions refer to the Clementi Sonatina movement that follows. Sonatina is the diminutive of sonata and is often applied to brief works in the form. Some sonatina movements have little or no development section, but this example, in spite of its extreme brevity, is perfectly proportioned.

1. Do a roman numeral analysis or macro analysis of the entire movement.
2. The exposition section is from measure 1 to measure _____.
3. The "development" section is from measure _____ to measure _____.
4. The recapitulation section is from measure _____ to measure _____.
5. The first theme is _____ measures in length.
6. The transition between the first and second themes is _____ measures in length.
7. The second theme is _____ measures in length.
8. The "development" is based on the _____ theme.
9. How does the recapitulation differ from the exposition?

Clementi: Sonatina, op. 36, no. 1 in C Major, I (Allegro).

The Classical Period (1750–1825)

Name _____

Section _____

Date _____

A. Refer to Beethoven's Piano Sonata in G Major, op. 49, no. 2 (II), on page 141. After listening to this composition, make a complete harmonic analysis. Then, on a separate sheet of paper:

1. Prepare a chart displaying the phrase-by-phrase analysis of the form.

2. As a part of the chart, show how the overall form is created from the phrase-by-phrase analysis.

3. Write a short paper of 200 to 400 words specifying information you learned from your analysis. Here are some ideas to help you get started. Indicate:

   a.   How the key relationships help to solidify the form of the movement.

   b.   Phrase lengths—generally similar or dissimilar in length.

   c.   Smaller forms within the overall form. Do phrases combine to form periods? Do periods combine to form double periods? Are any sections of the movement complete in themselves?

   d.   Any aspects of the form that depart from textbook descriptions.

   e.   Any harmony or harmonic progressions that were difficult for you to analyze. What about measures 9 and 10? Measures 42–46?

   f.   Any recurring melodic, harmonic, nonharmonic (such as pedal tones), or rhythmic features that tend to unify the work.

   g.   Compare general characteristics of this movement with others you have analyzed.

B. Refer to Haydn's Piano Sonata in D Major, Hob. XVI:19 (III), found on page 163. Complete the analysis of this movement following the same directions as found in section A above.

C. Refer to Beethoven's Piano Sonata in C Minor *(Pathétique)*, op. 13 (II), on page 128. Make an analysis using the same directions as in section A (this chapter) and compare the movement by Beethoven with the rondo in D Major by Haydn (see section B).

D. Write the first three sections of a five-part rondo form using the harmonic and melodic vocabulary of the late eighteenth century (classical period). Model the form after the first three sections (A B A) of the rondo in Piano Sonata in D Major by Haydn on page 163.

1. Write for the piano or any small group of instruments that are played by class members.

2. Use any of the following melodies in any combination you wish (you will need two). You will probably need to transpose them to fit the key relationships of the model.

3. If you wish, you may compose your own melodies, but be sure to show them to the instructor before proceeding with the composition.
4. Play the composition in class and have the students determine the overall form as well as the form of the various smaller sections.
E. Complete the remaining two sections of the five-part rondo begun in D. Continue to model your composition after the rondo in D Major by Haydn.

Play the completed composition in class. Have the class members choose some of the better works and schedule them for a student recital.

REVIEW

1. Review the outlines of the three-part, five-part, and seven-part rondos on page 154 of the text.
2. Examine figure 9.1 on page 155 in the textbook in detail, along with the summary discussion that follows. The rondo forms are very straightforward. The basic idea is that a single theme (called a refrain) is repeated a number of times, interspersed with contrasting materials (called episodes). Any composition with these properties can be called a rondo.

TEST YOURSELF 9

Answers are on page 228.

The following questions refer to the third movement from Clementi's Sonatina No. 5. This work, in spite of its extreme brevity, is a complete seven-part rondo.
1. Do a roman numeral analysis or macro analysis of the movement.
2. Identify the A theme (key will be important in determining the length of the theme).
3. Make an outline of the form. Include any transitions, retransitions, codettas, and coda in your outline.

Clementi: Sonatina, op. 36, no. 5 in G Major, III (Rondo).

The Classical Period (1750–1825)

10 9TH, 11TH, AND 13TH CHORDS

Name _____

Section _____

Date _____

A. Write the requested chord above each given note. The examples illustrate correct procedure.

1. Write a MmM 9th chord above each note (see measure 1 for an example).

1. (Ex.)   2.   3.   4.   5.   6.   7.   8.   9.   10.

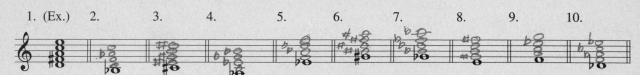

2. Write a Mmm 9th chord above each note (see measure 11 for an example).

11. (Ex.)   12.   13.   14.   15.   16.   17.   18.   19.   20.

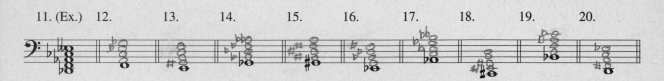

3. Write a dominant 11th chord above each note (see measure 21 for an example).

21. (Ex.)   22.   23.   24.   25.   26.   27.   28.   29.   30.

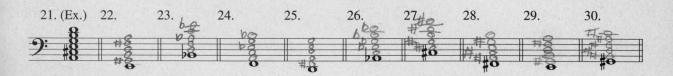

4. Write a dominant 11th chord with augmented 11th above each note (see measure 31 for an example).

31. (Ex.)   32.   33.   34.   35.   36.   37.   38.   39.   40.

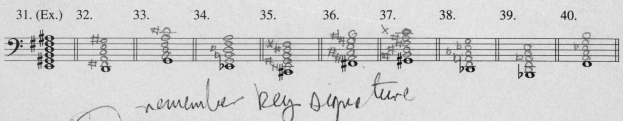

remember Key Signature

5. Write a dominant 13th chord above each note (see measure 41 for an example).

41. (Ex.)   42.   43.   44.   45.   46.   47.   48.   49.   50.

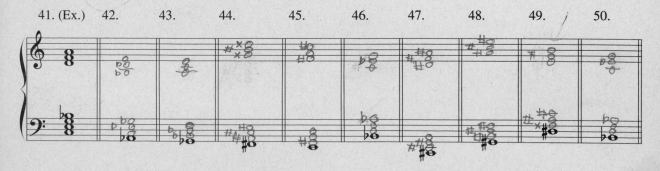

B. Reharmonize a popular song of your choosing.
   1. Select a popular song with which you are very familiar.
   2. On a separate sheet of paper, rewrite the melody line and the popular music chord symbols.
   3. Play over the melody several times using block chords and the popular music chord symbols given.
   4. Experiment with the harmony by keeping the basic chords as given, but make them into 9th, 11th, or 13th chords whenever the effect is desirable.
   5. When you have made your final selection of 9th, 11th, and 13th chords, change the block chords into a suitable accompaniment pattern for any instrument or group of instruments that can assure a performance in class.
   6. Perform the revised compositions in class. Have a voice major sing the melody line while accompanied by the instrument(s) of your choice.

C. Write a composition in *incipient three-part form.*
   1. Employ the following formal design:

Phrase	Key	Cadence	Relationship	Larger Form
1	B♭ Major	Half	a	A
2	B♭ Major Modulating to F Major	Authentic in F Major	ap	
3	F Major Modulating Back to B♭ Major	Half in B♭ Major	b	B
4	B♭ Major	Authentic	a'	A

   2. Arrange the harmonic vocabulary to contain no simple triads. Suggested chords are:
      a. 9th chords
      b. 11th chords
      c. 13th chords
      d. altered dominant 7th chords
      e. added 6th chords (triad plus interval of a 6th from root)
      f. 7th chords (any kind)
   3. Write for any instrument or instruments played by class members.
   4. Perform the compositions in class. Have the class select the best composition for a performance in a student recital.

D. Play or sing the following folk song melodies until you are entirely familiar with them before beginning the following exercises.
   1. Experiment with simple triadic harmony at the piano. At this point, play only block chords.
   2. On a separate sheet of paper, rewrite the melody and add the block harmony you think fits best.
   3. Add factors (7ths, 9ths, 11ths, and/or 13ths) to some of the existing chords, examining those that might add additional color to the accompaniment.
   4. Plan the accompaniment for a guitar, a piano, or an instrumental combo.
   5. With the block chords (now containing additional factors) as a basis, fashion an accompaniment pattern appropriate to the instrument(s) you selected.
   6. Write words of your own for each of the melodies. Place the words in the form of a *ballad* (a simple narrative poem made up of stanzas), one stanza for the sixteen measures printed. The same music is repeated for each stanza.
   7. Perform the works in class.

   Folk Song: "Barbara Allen."

Extended and Chromatic Harmony

Name _____

Section _____

Date _____

Folk Song: "Rising Sun."

E. Use suggested part-writing procedures discussed in the text.
1. Write from the figured bass the remaining three voices of each chord.
2. Name the key of each exercise.
3. Write the analysis of each chord in the blanks provided.

1.   2.   3.   4.

13	9		♮11	9		9	6		6	13
7	7		7	5		7	5			7
3	3		3	3		3	3			3

Analysis: ___ ___   ___ ___   ___ ___   ___ ___ ___

Key: _____   _____   _____   _____

5.   6.   7.

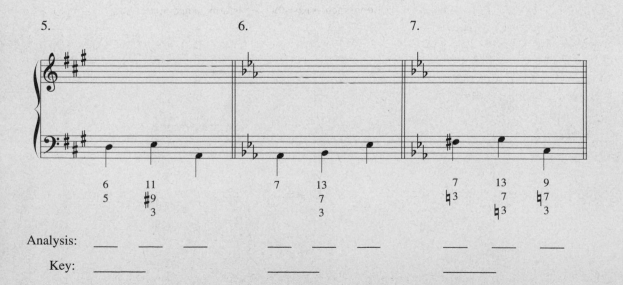

6	11		7	13		7	13	9
5	♯9			7		♮3	7	♮7
	3			3			♮3	3

Analysis: ___ ___ ___   ___ ___   ___ ___ ___

Key: _____   _____   _____

F. Following are four phrases. Add the alto and tenor voices according to the figured-bass or chord symbols.
   1. Numbers 1 through 3 contain figured-bass symbols; while in number 4, chord symbols are listed above the soprano voice.
   2. Generally when 9th, 11th, or 13th chords are called for (as in nos. 1–3), the figured-bass includes directions for all three voices above the bass. However, in a few instances (as in n. 1, chord 4), the missing factor is the interval of a diatonic 3rd above the bass.
   3. Note that in number 4 all chord symbols, except the last, call for dominant (or secondary dominant) chords. As an example, the "C♯¹³" refers to a C♯ dominant 13th chord, the "F♯⁹" indicates an F♯ dominant 9th, and so on. Make sure that you add whatever accidentals are needed to create the dominant sound.
   4. Also in number 4, it is suggested that the entire phrase be analyzed in the key of **G** Major.

Extended and Chromatic Harmony

4.

G. Following are three short melodies excerpted from popular songs by Duke Ellington.
1. Copy the melodies on score paper leaving three blank staves below each score of melody.
2. On the lowest (4th) staff, write out the chords in simple (closest) position.
3. On the two middle staves, compose a piano accompaniment.
   a. In the piano accompaniment, it is sometimes necessary (and desirable) to use chords in inversion for a smooth bass line and better voice leading.
   b. Because many of the chords are thick textured, it is wise to omit factors that would create excess dissonance and dense sonorities.
   c. The following illustrates one example of the first line of number 1:

Ellington: "Come Sunday."

4. Regarding the numbers above the chord symbols:
   a. At number 1, the soprano (**D**) creates a 13th above the root (**F**), but the chord symbol calls for a dominant-sounding 7th chord only.
   b. Similarly at number 2, the soprano (**A**) creates an 11th above the root (**E♭**), but the chord symbol calls for a dominant-sounding 9th chord.
   c. At numbers 3, 4, and 5, the bass note in the final two measures of the accompaniment should be **B♭**. **E♭/B♭** (n. 3) means to play an **E♭** Major triad with **B♭** as the bass note. Likewise, at number 4, the bass note should retain the **B♭**. The **B♭⁶** at number 5 means to play a **B♭** Major triad with an added sixth (**G**).
   d. At number 6, the melody note (**G♯**) is enharmonic with the chord symbol **A♭⁷**. Apparently, the composer considered **A♭⁷** to be simpler than **G♯⁷**.
   e. At number 7, the chord symbol is standard for a 13th chord with a minor 13th.
   f. At number 8, although the composer requests an **A♭¹³**, be careful how you employ the 13th in your accompaniment—avoid an excessively dissonant clash with the melody note.

Ellington: "Come Sunday."

Ellington: "Doin' the Crazy Walk."

Ellington: "Lady in Blue."

Extended and Chromatic Harmony

Name _____

Section _____

Date _____

H. Following are two short excerpts by Duke Ellington. Make a complete analysis of each.

1. Both excerpts abound in circle progressions and contain both 9th and 13th chords.
2. In "I Got It Bad," the circle progressions are clear and easy to identify. The final chord (measure 7B) is a major triad with an added 6th—the root is **G**.
3. In "Echoes of Harlem," measure 4 (which is repeated in measure 12) is an enigma. The chord (**G♭, B♭, D♭, F♭** [enharmonic with **E**]) is a tritone substitute for **C, E, G, B♭** and may be analyzed in at least two ways. An **A♭** major triad with an added 6th can be found in measures 8 and 18.

Ellington: " I Got It Bad."

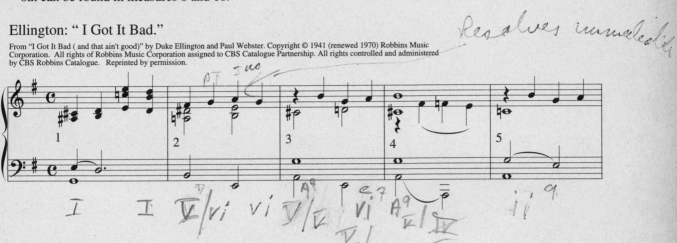

Ellington: "Echos of Harlem."

REVIEW

1. Spell the dominant 9th, 11th, and 13th chords in all major and minor keys. (Note that the 9th and 13th are major in the major keys and minor in the minor keys.)

2. Study figure 10.1 on page 165 of the textbook. Memorize the most common factors present in four-part settings of these chords and the voice-leading guides for each chord. Write dominant 9th, 11th, and 13th chords in a number of major and minor keys in four-part harmony and resolve each to its respective tonic triad using figure 10.2 as a guide.

3. If your instructor indicates that you should know the popular music chords symbols for the various 9th, 11th, and 13th chord qualities, study appendix B on page 317 of the textbook by playing each chord on the piano and transposing that chord to different roots. Pay particular attention to the popular music chord symbol for each chord.

TEST YOURSELF 10

Answers are on page 231.

All the following chords are secondary dominant 9th, 11th, or 13th chords.

1. Analyze each chord as a secondary dominant in two different keys and write the analysis in the blanks provided.
2. The example illustrates the correct procedure.

	Analysis	Key		Analysis	Key
1. (Ex.)	V⁹/V	B Major	6.	V¹¹	BM
	V⁹/ii	E Major			
2.	V¹³	AbM	7.	V⁹	C#M
3.	V¹¹	DM	8.	V¹¹	GM
4.	V¹³	EbM	9.	V¹³	DbM
5.	V⁹	AM	10.	V⁹	CM

II ALTERED DOMINANTS

Name _____

Section _____

Date _____

A. Each of the following chords is an altered dominant.
1. Write the correct analysis on the first blank beneath the staff.
2. Write the name of the key on the second blank beneath the staff.
3. The example illustrates the correct procedure.

+ - for fifth

1. (Ex.)   2.   3.   4.   5.   6.   7.   8.   9.   10.

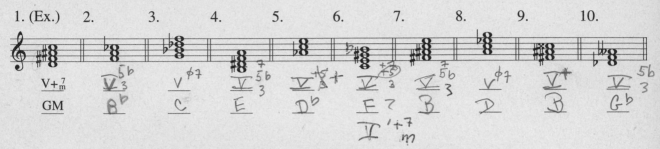

B. Each of the following tones represents the root of the altered dominant named directly beneath it.
1. On the staff, write the remaining tones of the requested chord.
2. The example illustrates the correct procedure.

11. (Ex.) 12.   13.   14.   15.   16.   17.   18.   19.   20.

11. (Ex.)	12.	13.	14.	15.	16.	17.	18.	19.	20.
$V+$	$V\flat^{7}_{53}$	$v^{\o 7}$	$V+^{7}$	$V^{\flat 5}_{3}$	$V+^{7}_{m}$	$V^{\flat 5}_{3}$	$v^{\o 7}$	$V+$	$V\natural^{7}_{53}$

C. Altered dominants may occur also as secondary altered dominants. Following are the analysis symbols and keys for ten such chords.
1. Write the requested secondary altered dominant on the staff in the blank measure provided.
2. The example illustrates the correct procedure.

Measure and Chord
21. V+/V in A Major
22. $V^{5\flat}$/V in Bb Major
23. $v^{\o 7}$/V in E Major
24. V^{+7}_{M}/V in G Major
25. $V^{7}_{5\flat}$/V in C Major

Measure and Chord
26. V+/IV in F Major
27. $V^{5\flat}$/VI in D Minor
28. $v^{\o 7}$/IV in D Major
29. V^{+7}_{M}/VI in G Minor
30. $V^{7}_{5\flat}$/IV in B Major

21. (Ex.) 22.   23.   24.   25.   26.   27.   28.   29.   30.

D. Add the alto and tenor voices and provide a harmonic analysis of each chord.

1.

2.

3.

4.

Extended and Chromatic Harmony

5.

E. Following are five phrases containing only a figured bass. These are similar in type to the assignment in chapter 4, section D, page 18.
1. Compose an appropriate soprano melody for each of the phrases.
2. Fill in the alto and tenor voices.
3. Make a complete harmonic analysis of each phrase.

F. Have a member of the class who is a piano major play the following excerpt.
    1. Do a roman numeral analysis and/or macro analysis of this excerpt.
    2. Discuss the use of altered dominants in the composition.
    3. Discuss the form of the work.
    4. Have one member of the class arrange the composition for four instruments played by class members. Play the work in class.
    5. Have those members who are not playing instruments swingle sing the excerpt, taking out-of-range tones up or down an octave as the need arises.

Beethoven: Bagatelle in C Major, op. 119, no. 8.

Extended and Chromatic Harmony

G. Compose the first sixteen measures of a popular song.

    1 . Use the following progressions or make up your own. If you decide to compose your own progressions, be sure to use a generous number of altered dominants.

       Upbeat: $G^{7(+5)}$

Measures	1:	C	C$\sharp$°	Measures	9:	C	C$\sharp$°
	2:	D$_{\text{MI}}^7$	D$\sharp$°		10:	D$_{\text{MI}}^7$	D$\sharp$°
	3:	E$_{\text{MI}}^7$			11:	E$_{\text{MI}}^7$	
	4:	A^7			12:	A^7	
	5:	D$_{\text{MI}}^7$	G^7		13:	D$_{\text{MI}}^7$	G^7
	6:	C			14:	C	E$_{\text{MI}}^7$ A^7
	7:	G$_{\text{MI}}^7$	A^7		15:	D$_{\text{MI}}^7$	G$^{7(-5)}$
	8:	D$_{\text{MI}}^7$	G^7 G^{7+5}		16:	C^6	

    2.   After selecting the progressions, write a melody to accompany.

    3.   Write your own lyrics to the song.

    4.   The accompaniment to the melody may be written for piano, guitar, or instrumental combo.

    5.   Arrange the block chords into an appropriate accompaniment figure.

    6.   Have a voice major sing the melodies with appropriate accompaniment in class.

REVIEW

1.   Study figure 11.1 (page 175 of the textbook), which shows the five altered dominant chords in common use. Choose a major key, spell the dominant 7th chord, and then alter it to make each of the five chords illustrated in figure 11.1. Repeat this process in several other keys.

2.   Study figure 11.4, which shows proper voice leading of altered dominant chords. Write each of the chords you spelled in number 1 above in four parts and resolve them properly to the tonic chord. Use the section titled "Voice Leading Altered Dominants" on page 176 for advice in proper voice leading.

TEST YOURSELF 11

Answers are on page 232.

1. Each of the following chords falls into one or two of the categories listed below. Identify each chord using the letters a, b, c, d, e, or f from the list below. If a chord could fit into two categories, give both letters.

   a. 9th, 11th, or 13th chord
   b. Neapolitan 6th chord — *Raise tonic ½ step + invert.*
   c. Augmented 6th chord
   d. Altered dominant — $V^+, V^{+7}, V^{5b}, V^7_{5b}, V^{\phi7}$
   e. Borrowed chord
   f. Secondary dominant

A. Write each of the six chromatic mediants in the following keys. The example illustrates the correct procedure.

1. (Ex.)

D Major: III   ♮III   ♮iii   VI   ♭VI   ♭vi

2.

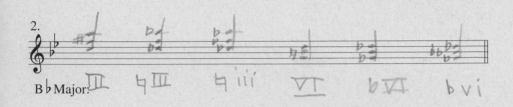

B♭ Major: III   ♮III   ♮iii   VI   ♭VI   ♭vi

3.

C Minor: iii   ♮♯III   ♮♯iii   vi   ♮✕VI   ♮✕vi

4.

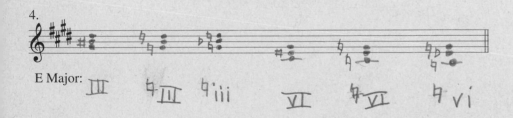

E Major: III   ♮III   ♮iii   VI   ♮VI   ♮vi

5.

D♭ Major: III   ♭III   ♭iii   VI   ♭VI   ♭vi

6.

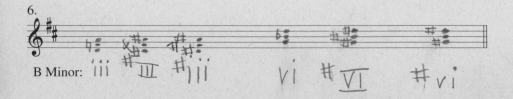

B Minor: iii   ♯III   ♯iii   vi   ♯VI   ♯vi

B. Add the alto and tenor voices and provide a harmonic analysis.

Extended and Chromatic Harmony

Name _____

Section _____

Date _____

C. Following are four phrases containing only a figured bass. These are similar in type to the assignment in chapter 4, section D, page 18.
1. Compose an appropriate soprano melody for each of the phrases.
2. Fill in the alto and tenor voices.
3. Make a complete harmonic analysis of each phrase.

D. Except for the first excerpt, each of the following melodies is a folk song.
1. Using the procedures outlined in chapter 10 of the textbook, volume 1, harmonize the folk songs, including at least one or two chromatic mediants in each.
2. Experiment by trying a fast (rapid change of chords), medium, and slow harmonic rhythm. Then select the one you prefer for each melody.
3. Write the accompaniment for guitar if the class has a guitar player. If the class has none, write for piano or small instrumental combo.
4. Write words of your own to each melody.
5. From the block chords of your original harmonization, fashion an accompaniment that fits the medium you choose (whether guitar, piano, or instrumental combo).
6. Perform the compositions in class. Have a vocal major sing the melodies.

Folk Song.

2.

Folk Song: Newfoundland.

3.

Folk Song: Kentucky.

4.

E. Write a short original composition of two to four phrases.
   1. Each phrase should be approximately four measures.
   2. Use only the harmonic vocabulary studied to date.
   3. Employ the following set of chord progressions or make up your own:

   GM: I ♭VI III I N⁶ V⁷ I ♭VI I III I iv I

   If you compose your own harmony, be sure you employ a generous number of chromatic mediants.
   4. Write for any group of instruments played by class members.
   5. Perform the compositions in class. Have the class critique each composition.
   6. If an electronic synthesizer is available to the class, have one member prepare his or her composition on tape. Play the tape in class.

REVIEW

1. Study figure 12.1 (page 179 of the textbook), which illustrates the six chromatic mediants in the major keys and the min keys (GM and em in the example). Choose a major key and spell all six chromatic mediant chords. Choose a minor key an spell the six chromatic mediant chords. Repeat this process in several other major and minor keys.
2. Chromatic mediants are most often approached or left by root motion of a 3rd, with chromatic motion in one or more part Study figure 12.3 to see these characteristics. Figure 12.2 illustrates the difference in function of the major triad on the 6 scale degree in major, which may be a secondary dominant of ii or a chromatic mediant, depending on the context. Stud this example carefully. Can a similar situation exist with any of the other chromatic mediant chords?

TEST YOURSELF 12

Answers are on page 232.

Write each of the six chromatic mediants in the following keys. The example in section 12A (page 81) illustrates the correct procedure.

1.
Eb Major: III bIII biii   VI bVI bvi

2.
Bb Minor: iii ♮iii ♮III   vi ♮vi ♮VI

3.
A Major: III ♮III ♮iii   VI ♮vi ♮VI

4.
Ab Major: III bIII iii   VI bvi bVI

5.
E Minor: iii #iii #III   vi #vi #VI

Name _____

Section _____

Date _____

A. Refer to Schubert's *Morgengrüss,* op. 89, no. 15, D. 975, on page 199. Have a voice major sing the composition.
  1. Make a complete harmonic analysis of the chords.
  2. On the score itself, circle all nonharmonic tones and name the type.
  3. Discuss the following:
     a.   The borrowed chords and their treatment
     b.   The harmonic rhythm—whether regular, irregular, fast, slow, etc.
  4. Arrange the accompaniment of the song for three or four instruments played by class members, and perform the work in class with a vocalist singing the vocal line.
B. Write a short *lied* of your own.
  1. Pattern the form and length after *Morgengrüss*.
  2. Be sure to include at least two borrowed chords in the composition.
  3. Either make up words of your own or select a short poem you particularly like.
  4. Perform the composition in class with a voice major singing the vocal line.
C. Have a piano major play each of the following excerpts in class. Analyze the works using the strategy suggested for section B above.

1. Mendelssohn: Sonata in G Minor, op. 105, II.

2. Tchaikovsky: *La Paupee Malade* (The Sick Doll) from Album for the Young, op. 39, no. 7.

D. Refer to Schubert's *Die Krahe* (The Crow) from *Winterreise* (Winter Journey), op. 89, no. 15, D. 911, on page 194. Make a complete harmonic analysis of this composition.

1. Discuss:
   a. The key scheme
   b. The form
   c. The number of phrases
   d. The cadence formulas
   e. Compositional devices such as sequences, repetition, etc.
   f. Harmonic rhythm
   g. Any other significant points regarding this composition
2. Have two students in the class perform the work, and then discuss pertinent items pertaining to interpretation and performance.

E. Have a member of the class who is a piano major play each of the following excerpts. Discuss the use of chromatic mediants in each excerpt.

Liszt: Apparitions no. 2.

molto ritenuto il Tempo

Liszt: *Un Sospiro* (A Sigh), no. 3 from *Trois Etudes de Concert* (Three Concert Etudes).

The Nineteenth and Twentieth Centuries

The following excerpt is the development section of a romantic-period sonatina. Analyze the excerpt, noting the following features:

1. In a few instances, weak key centers are established without reaching a tonic chord—dominant 7th chords are the only evidence of the new tonal center.
2. The excerpt contains no less than eight augmented 6th chords—some are repetitions.
3. Occasionally, an augmented 6th chord occurs in a nonconventional position, creating a diminished 3rd (the inversion of an augmented 6th).
4. Look carefully for upper pedal tones that are employed now and then. Such tones are not to be analyzed as components of the chords.

Schubert: Sonatina for Violin and Piano, op. 137, no. 2, D. 385.

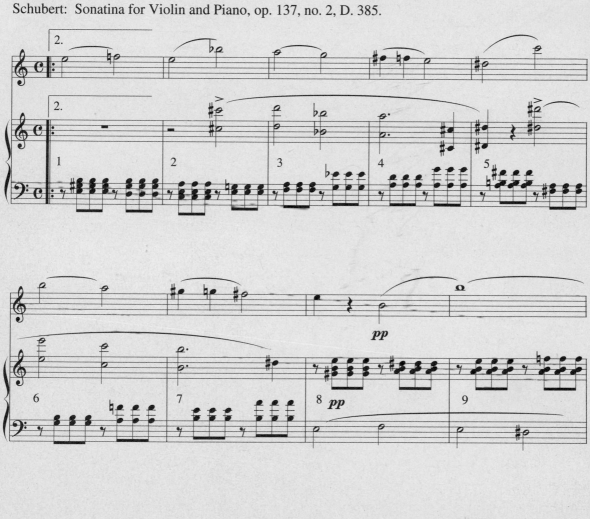

G. The following excerpt contains the first thirty-seven bars of Chopin's Nocturne, op. 48, no. 1. Analyze the excerpt, noting the following features:

1. A **ii⁰⁷** borrowed chord created through linear motion. Although not a prominent musical event in itself, when combined with several other altered chords produced through linear motion, a consistent stylistic pattern emerges.
2. A short fragment represented by the Neapolitan 6th chord along with its secondary dominant (dominant of the **N⁶**).
3. Another Neapolitan 6th chord (original key) that could also be analyzed as a submediant triad in another key.
4. A very brief **Fr⁶** (French augmented 6th) that proceeds to its dominant but does not continue on to tonic.
5. A momentary altered dominant (**V⁺⁷**) created through linear motion.
6. A curious chromatic mediant (**III**), arriving as expected from the tonic triad but progressing on to a supertonic 7th chord.

Chopin: Nocturne, op. 48, no. 1.

The Nineteenth and Twentieth Centuries

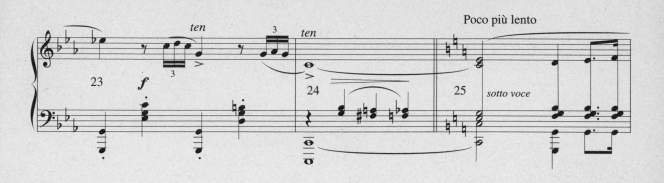

H. Refer to Chopin's Etude, op. 10, no. 2, on page 146. Listen to a recording of this work until you are familiar with it. This composition exhibits a steady stream of chromatic material, most of which is decoration.
   1. Analyze the underlying harmonic material, then compare the chords with the chromatic line above.
   2. Discuss the relationship between the two elements. Does the line always "fit" with the chords?
   3. Divide the work into phrases. What creates the sense of phrasing in this work?
   4. What elements of the romantic style are present in this work?

I. Refer to Clara Schumann's Variations on a Theme of Robert Schumann on page 202. This work is a good example of a theme and variation form as it occurred in the nineteenth century. Listen to this work until you are familiar with it.
   1. Analyze the theme in detail, noting any features that are characteristic of the romantic style.
   2. Compare each of the variations with the theme, noting the features that are varied and those that remain constant.
   3. Describe in detail the "new" materials in each variation. This may require harmonic analysis in some cases.
   4. Clara Schumann was married to Robert Schumann. Read biographical information on both composers in a music encyclopedia or the *Grove's Dictionary of Music*. Does this information shed any light on the background of this work?
   5. Write a short analytical paper presenting the results of your reading and analysis. Possible topics for such a paper include the following:
      a. The variation form in the romantic period
      b. Variation techniques used in this work
      c. Clara Schumann as pianist, composer, and wife, and the influence of each on the composition

REVIEW

1. Study figures 13.10 and 13.11 (page 194 of the textbook) and observe the enharmonic spelling of the diminished 7th chords. Write out four resolutions of chords "B" in figure 13.10, using figure 13.11 as a model. Now do the same for chord "C" in figure 13.10.

2. Select a major or minor key. Spell the dominant 7th chord in that key. Now respell the same chord enharmonically as a German 6th chord (only the 7th of the chord will need to be spelled enharmonically). In what key would you normally find that German 6th chord? The chord you spelled could be used as a pivot chord between those two keys. Choose another key and repeat the process.

3. Select a major or minor key. Spell the German 6th chord in that key. Now respell the same chord enharmonically as a dominant 7th chord (only the augmented 6th will need to be spelled enharmonically to form a minor 7th). In what key would you find the dominant 7th chord? The chord you spelled could be used as a pivot chord between those two keys. Repeat the process choosing another key.

4. Form a chart of the results of numbers 2 and 3 above. Do you see a pattern in the keys that can be related through the enharmonic relationship of the German 6th and the dominant 7th?

5. The following is a list of pairs of keys that are quite distant from each other. For each pair find at least three common chords between the keys. Consider diminished 7th chords, German 6th chords, Neapolitans, borrowed chords, and enharmonic spelling of diatonic triads in each key.

a. G Major	A♭ Major
b. E Major	B♭ Major
c. D Minor	D♭ Major
d. F♯ Major	B♭ Minor
e. A Minor	F♯ Major
f. F Major	C♯ Major

Test Yourself 13

Answers are on page 232.

Each of the following short excerpts contains a modulation in which the common chord is spelled enharmonically in one key. The enharmonic chord is marked by an asterisk in each excerpt. (There are two enharmonic chords in ex. 1. The second chord leads back to the original key.)
1.   Determine the two keys involved.
2.   Name the chord marked with an asterisk in both keys. (This will require an enharmonic spelling in one key.)

1. Chopin: Nocturne, op. 9, no. 1.

2. Haydn: String Quartet, op. 54, no. 1, Hob. III: 58.

3. Schubert: Waltz, op. 9, no. 14, D. 365.

4. Schubert: *Das Fischermädchen* (The Fishermaiden) from
   Schwangesang (Swan Song), D. 957, no. 10.

5. Chopin: Prelude, op. 28, no. 17.

14

The Post-Romantic, Impressionistic, and Related Styles

Name _____

Section _____

Date _____

A. Refer to Wolf's *In dem Schatten meiner Locken* on page 214. The text of this song is translated as follows:

> In the shadow of my tresses
> My beloved has fallen asleep.
> Shall I wake him?
> Ah no!
>
> With care I comb my curling
> Tresses daily at dawn,
> But in vain is my toil,
> For the winds blow them.
> Tresses' shadows and winds' blowing
> Have lulled my beloved to sleep.
> Shall I wake him?
> Ah no!
>
> I must hear how much he grieves,
> That he pines so long,
> That they give and take from him life—
> These my brown cheeks.
> And he calls me "Little Viper,"
> And yet falls asleep beside me.
> Shall I wake him?
> Ah no!

Have a singer prepare a performance of the song, or listen to a recording.
1. Analyze the chords using popular music chord symbols.
2. Mark all circle progressions in the song.
3. Note all chromatic third relationships between chords.
4. The key signature indicates B-flat Major or G Minor. Which is it? What other keys are established during the course of the song? Is there a pattern of key relationships?
5. Make a complete harmonic analysis, using roman numerals when appropriate and chord names in areas that are ambiguous as to key.
6. Trace repeated patterns in the accompaniment throughout the song. Are there repeated melodic patterns in the voice?
7. How is the meaning of the text expressed in the musical setting?
8. Write a short paper summarizing your findings.

B. Using the suggestions in the applications section of this chapter of the textbook (pages 225–226), do an analysis of the second movement of the *Sonatine* by Ravel (refer to page 189). Before preparing the analysis, have a student perform the composition several times in class or listen to a recording until the work is thoroughly familiar.

C. Refer to page 153. Make a complete analysis of *Danse sacrée,* which was written in 1904 by Debussy for harp and string orchestra.
   1. Use as a model the analysis in the text of *La Cathédrale engloutie* by Debussy.
   2. Include in your analysis a listing of any of the following devices of late nineteenth-century and early twentieth-century writing that occur in the composition:

Whole-tone scale	3rd relationship chords
Church modes	Parallel chords
Pentatonic scale	Traditional authentic cadences
Melodic doubling in parallel	Linear cadences
7th, 9th, 11th, and 13th chords	3rd relationship cadences
Chords of omission	Altered dominant or tonic cadences
Chords of addition	Other devices
Quartal chords	

   3. Make an analysis of the form of the composition.
   4. Before beginning the analysis, listen to a recording of the composition. If a member of the class plays the harp, ask her or him to demonstrate the instrument, explain the use of the pedals, and provide some information about writing for the harp.
D. Use as the theme the tune "America" (or any well-known melody of about the same length) and write a series of five variations.
   1. Begin with the theme stated simply with harmonic accompaniment as you usually hear it.
   2. Write each of the five variations employing the complete melody in the following manner:
      a. *First Variation:* Put the melody in the Dorian mode and highlight it with a number of planed triads or 7th chords.
      b. *Second Variation:* Place the melody into the framework of a whole-tone scale and accompany it with a short ostinato figure utilizing tones of the same whole-tone scale.
      c. *Third Variation:* Rework the meter of the melody employing changing meters. Maintain an accompaniment that contains a majority of quartal chords.
      d. *Fourth Variation:* Make the melody fit into a pentatonic scale (example: C D E G A) with a harmonic accompaniment emphasizing 3rd-relationship chords.
      e. *Fifth Variation:* Retain the melody in the major mode but change the note values of the tones. Emphasize a rich harmonic background made up of a majority of 9th, 11th, and 13th chords.
   3. Write for any instrument or combination of instruments played by class members.
   4. Play the composition in class. As a term project, have some class members arrange their compositions for a large ensemble, such as wind ensemble, band, or orchestra. Ask the conductor of the appropriate large ensemble in your school to give the compositions a reading at a rehearsal session.
E. Have a member of the class who is a piano major play the following excerpt.
   1. Extract the chords and write them in simple position on the blank staves beneath the score.
   2. Discuss the use of altered dominants.

MacDowell: "Moonshine" from Four Little Poems for Piano, op. 32.

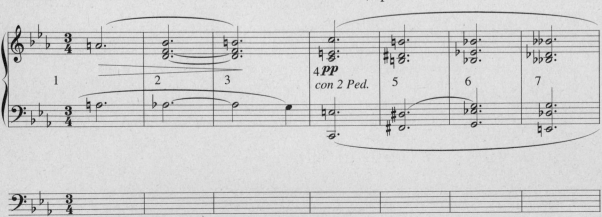

The Nineteenth and Twentieth Centuries

Name ______________________

Section ______________________

Date ______________________

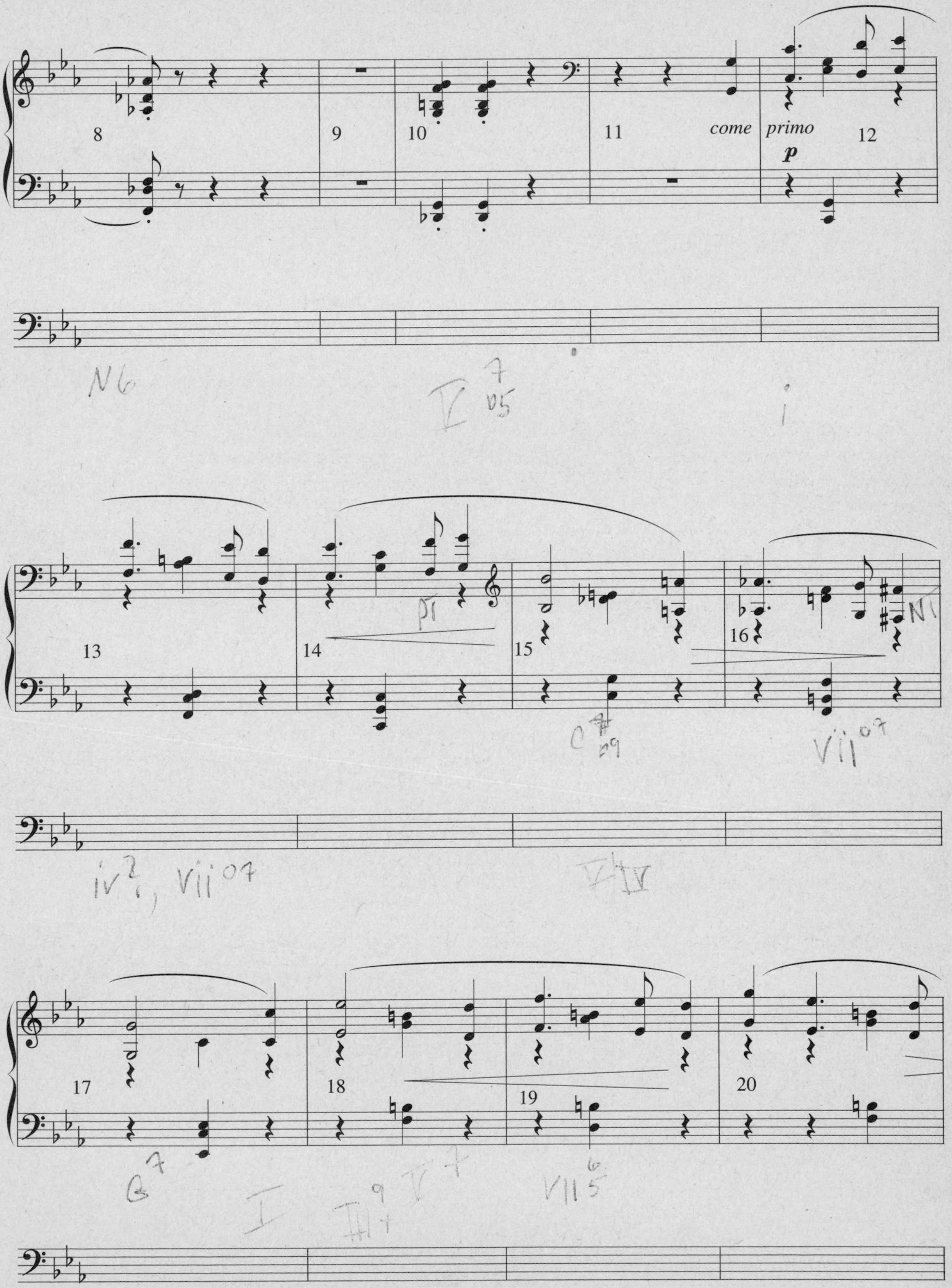

The Nineteenth and Twentieth Centuries

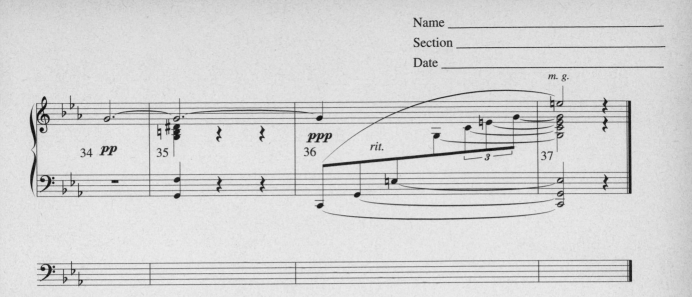

F. Have a member of the class who is a piano major play each of the following excerpts.
1. Extract the chords and write them in simple position on the blank staves beneath each score.
2. Discuss the use of chromatic mediants in each excerpt.

Debussy: Nocturne in D-flat Major.

Debussy: *Fêtes* (Festivals) from Nocturnes (Arrangement of Orchestral Work).

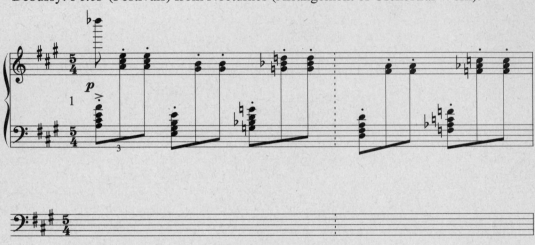

The Nineteenth and Twentieth Centuries

Name _____

Section _____

Date _____

REVIEW

1. Study the list of terms at the beginning of chapter 14 (page 207 of the textbook). Define each of the terms in your own words. Take a piece of paper and make three headings: **Post Romanticism, Impressionism,** and **Both.** Place each term on the list under one heading, depending on the style to which that term refers. (Place a term in the **Both** column if it refers to a characteristic of both styles.)

2. Review the authentic form of the church modes (see figures 2.30 and 2.32 on pages 44 and 45 in volume 1 of the textbook). Select a single note. Spell each of the modes beginning on that note. Repeat this process using a different note.

3. Study figure 14.10 on page 214 of the textbook which shows two common pentatonic scales. Write these two pentatonic scales beginning on several different notes.

4. Spell the whole-tone scale beginning on several notes.

5. Study figure 14.21, which shows a number of consonant and dissonant quartal chords, all spelled beginning on A. Spell these chords beginning on several other notes.

6. Carefully examine the specimen analysis (figure 14.37 on page 226 of the textbook) after listening to the work several times. See if you understand each analytical symbol.

7. Review the Suggested Approach to Analysis on pages 225–226 of the textbook. This step-by-step procedure will help you to establish an organized approach to analysis.

TEST YOURSELF 14

Answers are on page 233.

Play the excerpt from Franck: Chorale for Organ no. 2 several times (or listen to a recording) and then answer each of the following questions:

1. Is the scale basis diatonic or chromatic?
2. Do an analysis of this excerpt. Show the key signature, time signature and eight blank measures. Examine the harmonic vocabulary by writing each chord on the analysis line (the harmonic rhythm is given above the staff). Label each chord using popular-music chord symbols. What is the most common chord quality in this excerpt?
3. List pairs of chords that could be functionally related to each other and give a key and possible roman numeral for each chord. Do any of these progressions result in the establishment of a tonal center?
4. Are there any progressions in which nonfunctional harmony is organized around a chromatic step progression?
5. Point out three places where accented nonharmonic tones increase the level of dissonance.

Franck: Chorale for Organ, no. 2, mm. 39–46.

The following are short excerpts from the works of impressionistic composers. Using the following list, identify elements in each excerpt that are characteristic of impressionistic style.

a. Church modes
b. Pentatonic scale
c. Whole-tone scale
d. 9th, 11th, and 13th chords
e. Chords of addition and omission
f. Quartal/quintal chords
g. Linear cadence
h. 3rd-relationship cadence
i. Melodic doubling at various intervals
j. Parallel chords (planing)

1. Debussy: *La Cathédrale engloutie* (The Engulfed Cathedral), no. 10 from Preludes, Book I.

2. Debussy: *Pelléas et Mélisande,* Act I, scene I.

3. Debussy: *Canope* (Canopic Jar), no. 10 from Preludes, Book II.

4. Ravel: *L'Enfant et Les Sortilèges* (The Child and His Fantasies).

5. Debussy: Nocturnes, *Fêtes*.

Name _____

Section _____

Date _____

A. This section refers to five short compositions or excerpts. For convenience, the following list includes some (but not all) twentieth-century musical devices:

Melodic doubling in parallel

7th, 9th, 11th, and/or 13th chords

Chords of omission or addition

Quartal chords

3rd relationship of chord roots

Parallel chords

Synthetic scales

Polytonality

Polychords

Free tonality

Pandiatonicism — *equality of all notes no leading tone*

Ostinato

Polyrhythm

Modal scales

1. Determine the relationship between the lower-voice melody and the chordal figures above it. What twentieth-century device is most prominent here?

Kabalevsky: Toccatina, op. 27.

Source: Benjamin/Horvip/Nelson: Music for Analysis. © 1978 Houghton Mifflin, Boston, MA

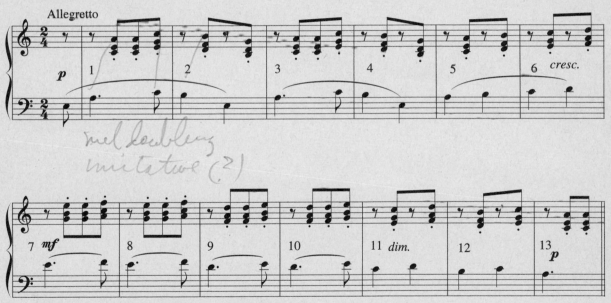

mel doubling imitative (?)

2. Refer to Lutoslawski's Bucolic no. 2 on page 179. This short work lends itself best to the analytical procedures used on Bartók's Chromatic Invention no. 91 (figure 15.36) in chapter 15 of the textbook. Make a complete analysis of the composition from that viewpoint.

3. Refer to Schuman's No. 2 from Three Score Set on page 201. At least two twentieth-century devices are obvious in this composition. Other relationships as well should be investigated. Make a list of these.

4. Somewhat more complicated is this excerpt from an early bagatelle by Bartók. More than one approach may be required to explain its patterned relationships.

Bartók: No. 11 from Fourteen Bagatelles, op. 6, m. 1-39.

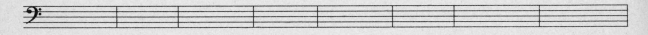

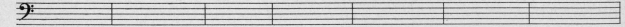

The Nineteenth and Twentieth Centuries

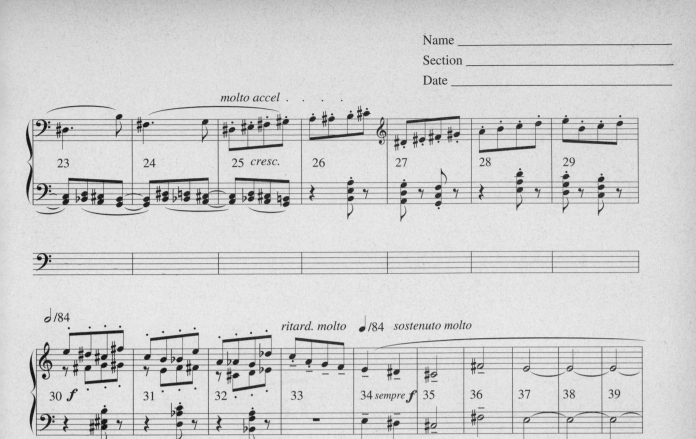

5. The tonal relationships found in this Prelude by Shostakovich are quite different from those of the eighteenth and nineteenth centuries, but a harmonic analysis might be the best way to begin.

Shostakovich: Prelude, op. 34, no. 24.

Allegretto

B. Persichetti's "March" from Divertimento for Band is reprinted on page 186 in a simplified score form for purposes of space conservation.

1. From the following list, select devices found in this composition:

Melodic doubling in parallel   Polytonality
7th, 9th, 11th, and/or 13th chords   Polychords
Chords of omission or addition   Free tonality
Quartal chords   Pandiatonicism
3rd relationship of chord roots   Ostinato
Parallel chords   Polyrhythm

2. List any other musical relationships or devices that cannot be described by any of the preceding terms.
3. Determine the form of the composition, and indicate the unifying factors that hold this work together.

C. Listen to a recording of the first twelve measures of *Danse Russe* and, on a separate sheet of manuscript paper, reduce the full score to one that can be played on one or two pianos.

1. From the following list of twentieth-century devices, determine which one is the most evident:

Melodic doubling in parallel   Polytonality
7th, 9th, 11th, and/or 13th chords   Polychords
Chords of omission or addition   Free tonality
Quartal chords   Pandiatonicism
3rd relationship of chord roots   Ostinato
Parallel chords   Polyrhythm

2. List any other devices you can find in this short excerpt.
3. If you find other musical relationships or devices that cannot be described by any of the preceding terms, write them down using your own descriptive terms.

Name ______________________________

Section ______________________________

Date ______________________________

Stravinsky: *Danse Russe* (Russian Dance) from *Petrouchka.*

REVIEW

1. Use the list of terms on page 243 of the textbook as a test of your understanding of the materials of contemporary music. Define each term in your own words, and check your definitions with the definitions in the book.

2. Write a number of polychords using major and minor triads at different intervals (use figures 15.6 and 15.7 on pages 246–247 of the textbook as models). Test each at the piano to compare the levels of dissonance among your polychords.

3. Select four notes at random or choose a motive from a composition you are studying. Find the normal order (or best normal order) for this tetrachord (see figures 15.32–15.35). Now write the inversion of this set (see figures 15.28–15.30). Select other groups of three, four, and five notes for similar treatment. Play each set and its inversion to hear the similarity between them.

4. Study the specimen analyses (figures 15.16 and 15.36) carefully, making certain that you understand each label.

TEST YOURSELF 15

Answers are on page 233.

The following are short excerpts from the works of contemporary composers. Identify elements in each excerpt that are characteristic of the contemporary period, using the following list:

a. Pandiatonicism
b. Polytonality
c. Dual modality
d. Shifted tonality
e. Free tonality
f. Polychords
g. Quartal/quintal chords
h. Clusters
i. Changing meter
j. Asymmetric meter
k. Nonaccentual rhythms

1. Poulenc: "Laudamus Te" from Gloria.

2. Ives: "Lincoln, the Great Commoner" (No. 11 of 114 Songs).

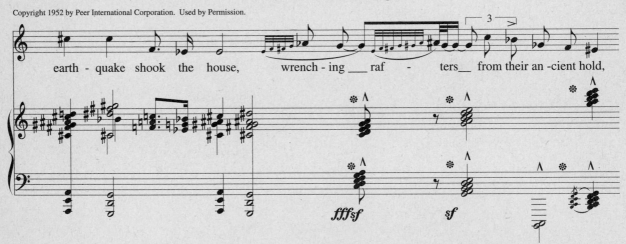

3. Bartók: Bagatelle I.

4. Honegger: Symphony No. 5, "Di tre re," I.

5. Ives: Second Sonata for Violin and Piano, III.

Examine each of the following short melodic fragments and derive a set that includes all the pitch classes present in the melody. Place this set in normal order.

6.

7.

8.

16 TWELVE-TONE TECHNIQUE

Name _____

Section _____

Date _____

A. Refer to Krenek's Etude from Eight Piano Pieces, 1946, on page 174. Have a pianist play this work or listen to a recording.
  1. Find the row, which is stated in the first three measures of the right hand.
  2. Make a matrix for this row using the instructions in chapter 16 of the textbook.
  3. Analyze the pitch content of the work by labeling all the row forms and numbering the pitches.
  4. Describe how the row is used in this work. What is the basic texture?
  5. How does the row influence phrasing and form?
  6. Make an arrangement of this work for four woodwind or string instruments. Perform the arrangement in class. Compare your arrangement to the original piano form. Which best expresses the ideas of the piece?

REVIEW

1. Write a twelve-tone row of your own choosing. (Choose notes at random if you prefer.) Create a matrix for this row using the instructions on pages 280–282 of the textbook. Write a melodic line using two forms of the row.
2. Study the specimen analysis (figure 16.1 on pages 274–280 of the textbook), making certain that you understand each analytical symbol.
3. Define each of the terms at the head of the chapter (page 277 of the textbook) in your own words. Check your definitions with the definitions in the chapter.

TEST YOURSELF 16

Answers are on page 234.

The following composition is written in serial technique. Find the row (in the first five measures of the voice) and form a matrix. Do a serial analysis along the lines of the specimen analysis in this chapter (figure 16. 1).

Dallapiccola: *Goethe-Lieder,* no. 2, for Mezzo-Soprano and E-flat Clarinet.

By permission of Edizioni Suvini Zerboni, Milano.

* *La parte del Clar. picc. è scritta in suoni reali.*
(The E-flat Clarinet part is written at sounding pitch.)

Anthology

Name _____

Section _____

Date _____

Bach: Fugue no. 7 in E-flat Major, BWV 852 from The Well-Tempered Clavier, Book 1.

Anthology

Bach: Invention no. 1 in C Major BWV 772 from Fifteen Two-Part Inventions.

Beethoven: Sonata in C Minor *(Pathétique),* op. 13, II.

Name ______________________________

Section ______________________________

Date ______________________________

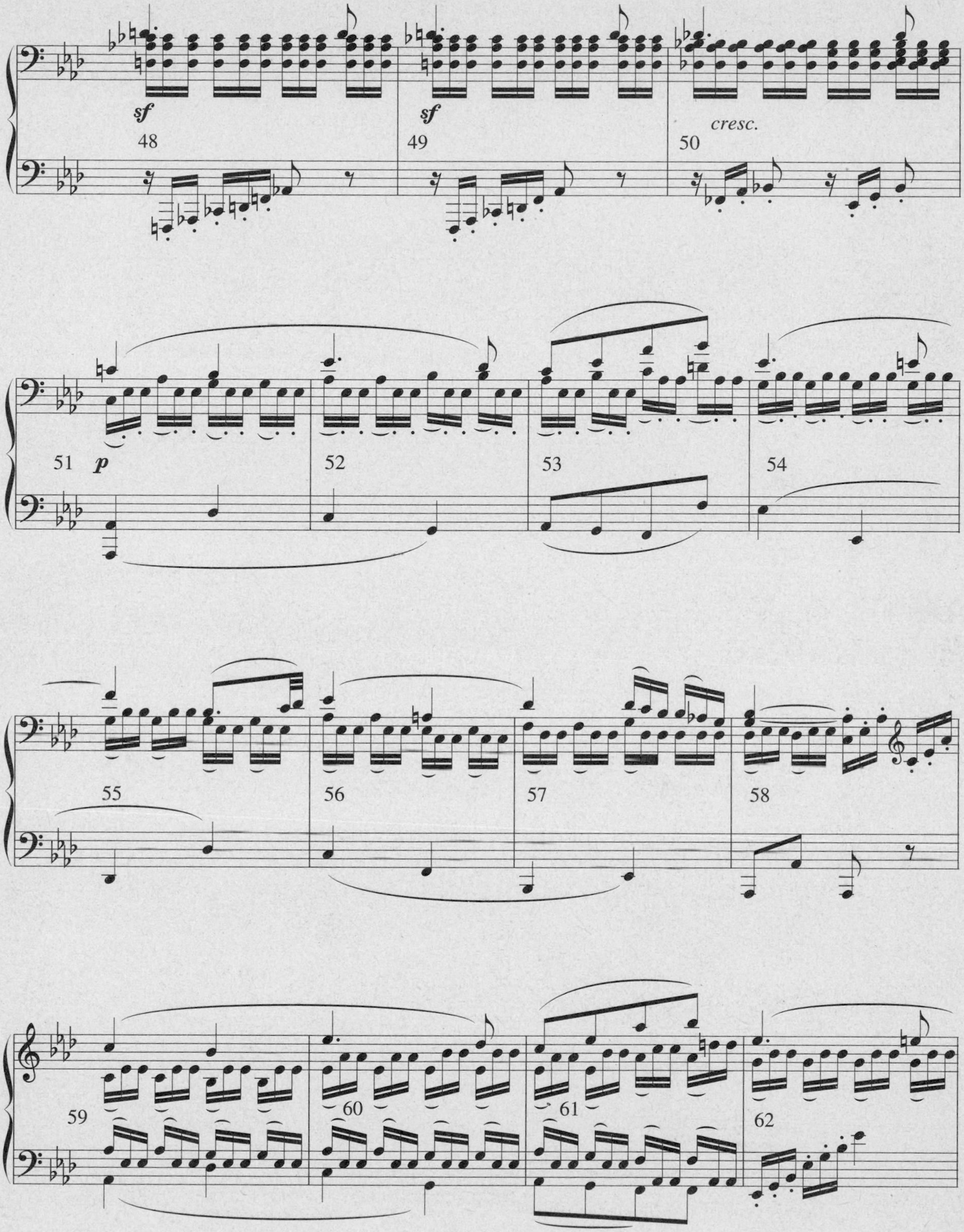

Beethoven: Sonata in G Major, op. 14, no. 2, I.

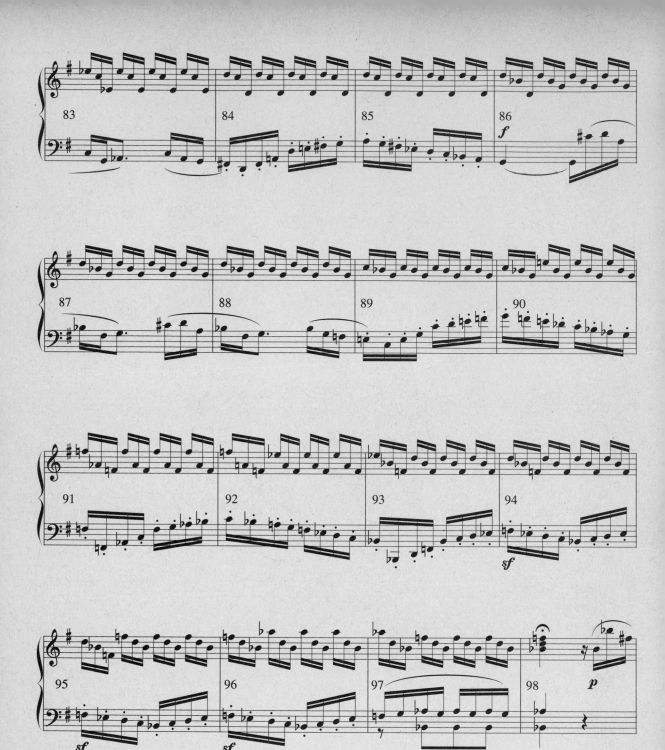

Anthology

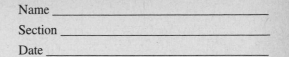

Beethoven: Sonata in G Major, op. 49, no. 2, II.

Tempo di Menuetto (♩ = 112)

Anthology

Chopin: Etude, op. 10, no. 2.

Name_____

Section_____

Date_____

Debussy: *Danse sacrée* (Sacred Dance) for harp and string orchestra.

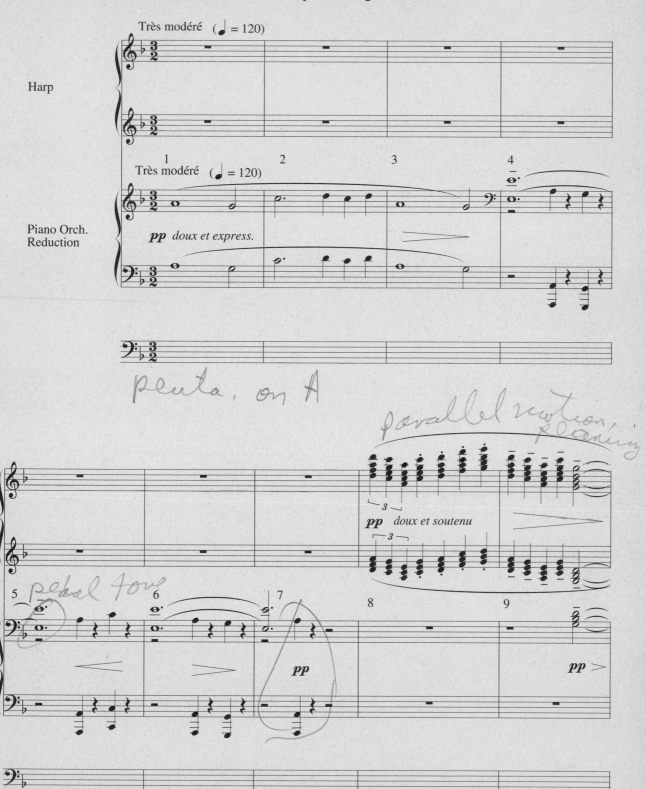

whole tone vs chromatic

En animant peu à peu

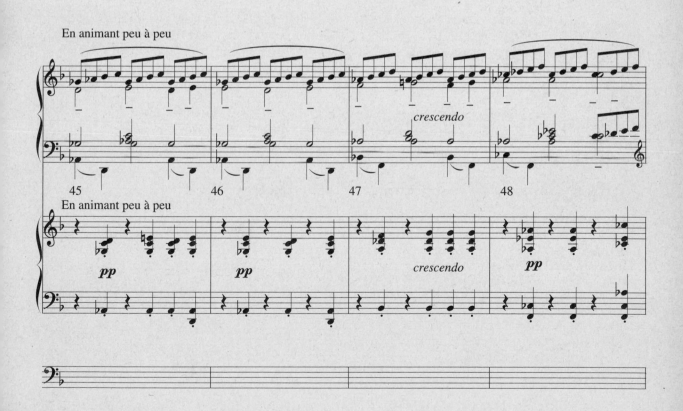

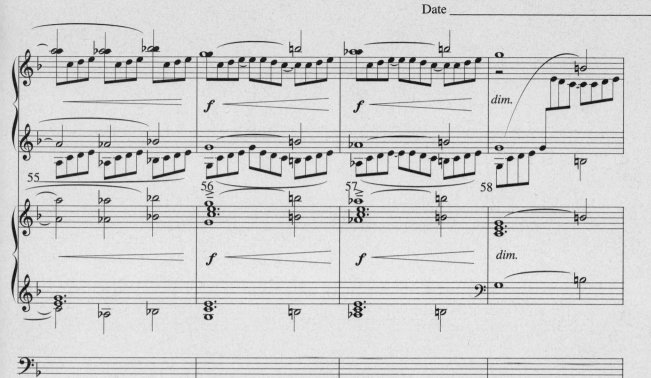

3rd relationship, melodic doubling

quantile chords (4ths)

Haydn: Sonata in D Major, Hob. XVI:19, III.

Haydn: Sonata in G Major, Hob. XVI: 27, I.

Allegro con brio

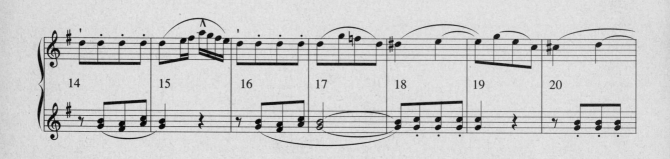

Krenek: Etude from Eight Piano Pieces, 1946.

Lassus: *Missa pro defunctis,* Benedictus.

Lassus: *Sancta mei.*

- - bis, e - go red - dam vo - - - - bis.

- - bis, e - go e - go red - dam vo - - - - bis.

Lassus: *Sicut rosa.*

Tenor

Sic - - - - ut ro - - - sa, sic - ut

Bassus

Sic - ut ro - - - - sa, sic - -

ro - - - sa in - - - ter spi - nas il - las

- ut ro - - sa - - ter spi - - nas
in

au - dit spe - - - - - ci - em, sic re - nu - stat su -

il - las au - dit spe - - - ci - em, sic re -

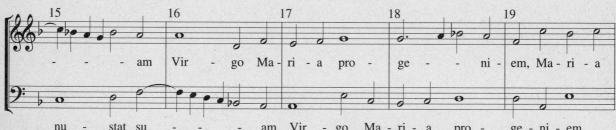

- - - am Vir - go Ma - ri - a pro - ge - - ni - em, Ma - ri - a

nu - stat su - - - am Vir - go Ma - ri - a pro - ge - ni - em,

pro - ge - - - - - - - ni - em: ger - mi - na - - vit e -

Ma - ri - a pro - - ge - ni - em: ger - mi - na - vit e - nim flo -

Lutoslawski: Bucolic no. 2.

Copyright Polskie Wydawnictwo Muzyczne, Krakow, Poland. Reprinted by permission.

Mozart: Sonata in G Major, K. 283, I.

　　　　　Anthology

codetta

Development - what themes
codetta are developed

end of exposition

IX Development of theme I

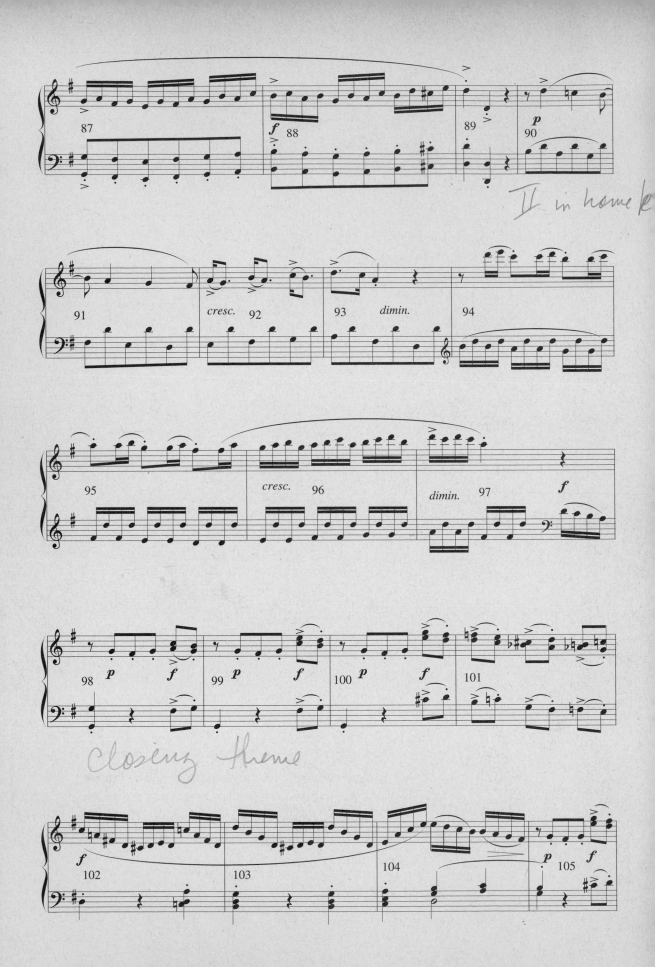

II in home k

closing theme

name key-codetta

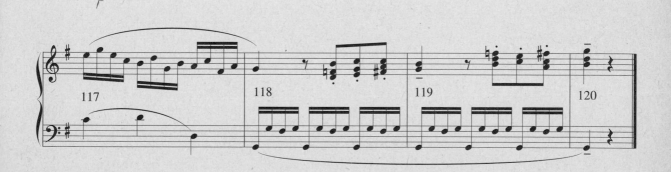

Persichetti: "March" from divertimento for band.

Anthology

Ravel: Sonatine, II.

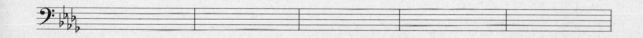

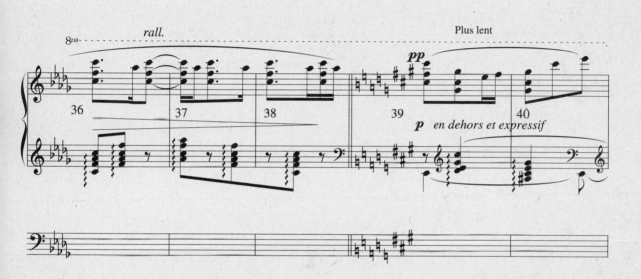

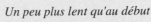

Un peu plus lent qu'au début

ralentissez beaucoup -

Schubert: *Die Krähe* (The Crow) from *Winterreise* (Winter Journey), op. 89, no. 15, D. 911.

war mit mir aus der Stadt ge - zo - - gen,

ist bis heu - te für und für um mein Haupt ge -

flo - gen.

Krä - he,   wun-der-liches Thier,   willst mich nicht ver -

las - sen?   Meinst wohl   bald als Beu - - te hier

cresc.

mei - nen Leib zu fas - sen?

Nun es wird nicht weit mehr geh'n an dem Wan - der -

sta - - be, Krä - he, lass' mich end - lich seh'n

cre - scen - - do

Treu - e bis zum Gra - - - be!

Krä - - he, lass' mich end - lich seh'n Treu - - e bis zum

Gra - - - - be!

Schubert: *Morgengrüss* (Greeting) from *Die schöne Müllerin* (The Miller's Beautiful Daughter), op. 25, no. 8, D. 795.

Gu - ten Mor - gen, schö - ne
O lass mich nur von
Ihr schlum - mer - trunk'nen
Nun schüt - telt ab der

Mül - le - rin! wo steckst du gleich das Köpf - chen hin, als wär' dir was ge - sche - hen? Ver -
fer - ne steh'n, nach dei - nem lie - ben Fen - ster seh'n, von fer - ne, ganz von fer - ne! Du
Äu - ge - lein, ihr thau - be - trüb - ten Blü - me - lein, was scheu - et ihr die Son - ne? Hat
Traü - me Flor, und hebt euch frisch und frei em - por in Got - tes hel - len Mor - gen! Die

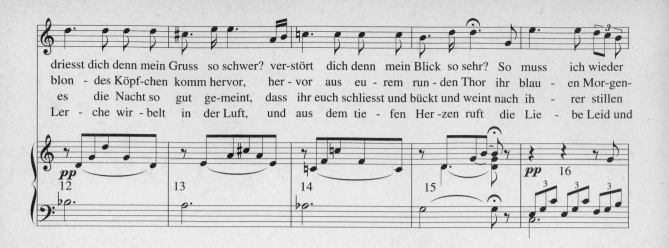

driesst dich denn mein Gruss so schwer? ver-stört dich denn mein Blick so sehr? So muss ich wieder
blon - des Köpf-chen komm hervor, her - vor aus eu - rem run - den Thor ihr blau - en Mor-gen-
es die Nacht so gut ge-meint, dass ihr euch schliesst und bückt und weint nach ih - rer stillen
Ler - che wir-belt in der Luft, und aus dem tie - fen Her -zen ruft die Lie - be Leid und

ge - hen, so muss ich wie-der ge - hen, wie-der ge - hen.
ster - ne, ihr blau - en Mor-gen-ster - ne, ihr Mor-gen-ster - ne!
Won - ne, nach ih - rer stil-len Won - ne, nach ih - rer Won - ne?
Sor - gen, die Lie - - be Leid und Sor - gen, Leid und Sor - gen.

Schuman: No. 2 from Three Score Set.

Used by permission of G. Schirmer, Inc. Copyright © 1943 G. Schirmer, Inc.

Schumann, Clara: Variations on a Theme of Robert Schumann, op. 20.

Variation II

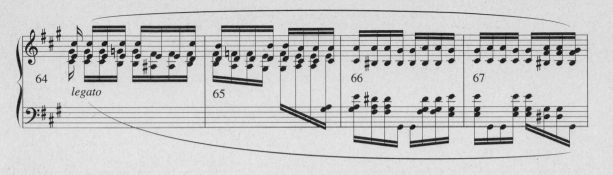

Variation III

Variation IV

Variation V

Anthology

Variation VII

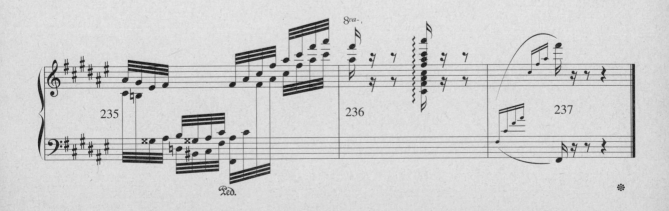

Wolf: *In dem Schatten meiner Locken* (In the Shadow of My Curls) from *Spanisches Liederbuch.*

strählt' ich mei - ne kraus-en Lo - cken täg - lich in der Frü - he,

doch um-sonst ist mei-ne Mü - he, weil die Win - - de sie zer-

sau - sen. Lo-cken-schat - ten,

Win-des - sau - sen schlä - fer - ten den Lieb - sten ein,

Weck' ich ihn nun auf? _____ Ach

nein! Hö - ren muss ich, wie ihn grä - me, dass er

schmach - - tet schon so lan - - ge, dass ihm Le - ben geb' und

neh - me die - se mei - ne brau - ne Wan - - - ge.

Und er nennt mich sei - ne

Schlan - ge, und doch schlief er bei__ mir ein.

Weck' ich ihn nun auf?_____ Ach nein!____

Answers to Self–Tests

Test Yourself 1 (page 4)

1–3. Lassus:*Justus cor suum tradet.*

4. To avoid the **F– B♮** tritone
5. There are no deviations.
6. 11
7. Dorian

2. motive
3. motive, 11th (8ve + 4th), countermotive
4. sequence
5. 14, dominant
6. motive, tonic
8. 3

7. Bach: Invention no. 10, BWV 781, in G Major, from Fifteen Two-Part Inventions.

TEST YOURSELF 3 (PAGE 11)

1. Tonal. Second note (and following notes) are P4 rather than P5 above subject. The strong tonic–dominant opening of the subject is answered by dominant–tonic.
2. Real
3. Tonal. Second measure (and following) of subject is answered tonally (P5 below rather than P4). The subject modulates to the dominant key.

4. Bach: Fugue in D Minor, BWV 899.

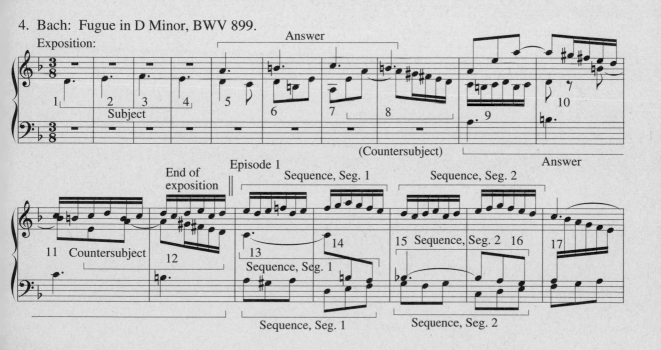

Answers to Self-Tests

Test Yourself 4 (page 19)

EbM: ii°6   V   F#M: ii°$^4_3$ V   EM: iv   V$^4_3$ F#M: bVI   V   BM: vii°7   I

DM: iv6   V   F#M: vii°7   I   AbM: bVI   V   CM: ii°$^6_5$ V   C#M: bVI6   V$^6_5$

Test Yourself 5 (page 30)

bbm: N6   V   f#m: N6   V   em: N6   V

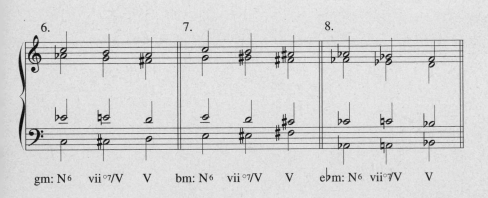

gm: N6   vii°7/V   V   bm: N6   vii°7/V   V   ebm: N6   vii°7/V   V

gm: N⁶   i⁶₄   V   bm: N⁶   i⁶₄   V   fm: N⁶   i⁶₄   V

Test Yourself 6 (page 38)

1. bm: Gr⁶   i⁶₄   2. gm: Gr⁶   i⁶₄   3. CM: Fr⁶   V   4. B♭M: It⁶   V   5. EM: Fr⁶   V

6. F♯M: It⁶   V   7. dm: Gr⁶   i⁶₄   8. FM: Gr⁶   I⁶₄   9. AM: Fr⁶   V   10. g♯m: Gr⁶   i⁶₄

Test Yourself 7 (page 53)

2. Variation I

Variation techniques:
Embellished melodic line.

3. Variation II

legato

Variation techniques:
Change of accompaniment texture.

4. Variation V

p

Variation techniques:
Introduction of a unique rhythmic figure.

5. Variation VII

f

Variation techniques:
Embellished melodic line.
Extending the range of the melody.

6. Variation VIII

Variation techniques:
Change of mode.
Embellished melodic line.
Treating a motive from the melody (embellished) in imitation.

7. Variation XI

Variation techniques:
Change of tempo.
Embellished melodic line.
Treating a motive from the melody (embellished) in imitation.
Change of accompaniment texture.

8. Variation XII

Variation techniques:
Change of meter.
Embellished melodic line.
Change of accompaniment texture.

1. Clementi: Sonatina, op. 36, no. 1 in C Major, I (Allegro).

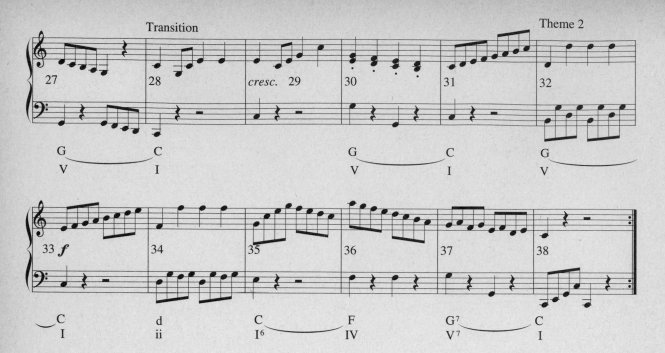

2. 15
3. measure 16 to measure 23
4. measure 24 to measure 38
5. 4
6. 4
7. 7
8. first
9. The second theme is in the tonic key.

Test Yourself 9 (page 62)

Clementi: Sonatina, op. 36, no. 5 in G Major, III (Rondo).

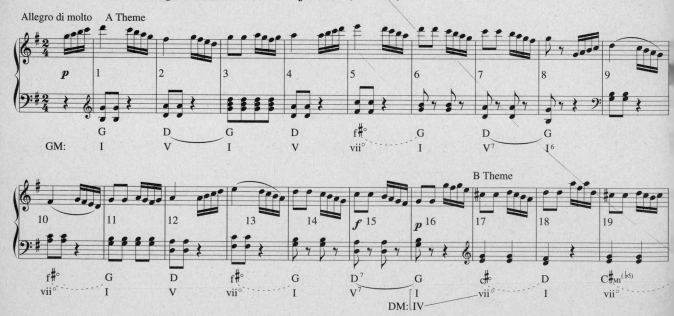

Section	Phrase	Measure	Key	Cadence
...ection	1	1–4	GM	H
	2	5–8	GM	IA
	3	9–12	GM	H
	4	13–16	GM	PA
...o transition				
	5	17–20	DM	IA
	6	21–24	DM	PA
...etransition	7	25–28	to GM	H
...A	8	29–32	GM	H
	9	33–36	GM	IA
	10	37–40	GM	H
	11	41–44	GM	PA
...odetta	12	45–52	GM	PA
	13	53–58	GM	PA
...o transition				
...C	14	59–62	em	H
	15	63–66	to bm	H
	16	67–70	bm	H
	17	71–74	to AM	PA
	18	75–84	to DM	PA
	19	85–94	DM	PA
	20	95–102	DM	PA
...odetta	21	103–106	DM	PA
...etransition	22	107–113	to GM	H

Da Capo completes the form: **A B A C A B A**

TEST YOURSELF 10 (PAGE 73)

The following are some possible answers. In many cases you may have chosen other answers.

Analysis	Key	Analysis	Key
(Ex.) 1. V^9/V	B Major	6. V^{11}/ii	A Major
V^9/ii	E Major	V^{11}/vi	D Major
2. V^{13}/V	D♭ Major	7. V^9/V	f♯ Minor
V^{13}/ii	G♭ Major	V^9/iii	A Major
3. V^{11}/ii	C Major	8. V^{11}/V	C Major
V^{11}/vi	F Major	V^{11}/IV	D Major
4. V^{13}/V	A♭ Major	9. V^{13}/III	b♭ Minor
V^{13}/III	C Minor	V^{13}/V	G♭ Major
5. V^9/IV	E Major	10. V^9/VI	e Minor
V^9/V	D Major	V^9/V	F Major

(Ex.)	1. f	6. c	11. b,e	16. e
	2. b,e	7. d	12. c	17. a
	3. d	8. f	13. c,d	18. f
	4. c	9. c	14. c,d	19. e,f
	5. e	10. a	15. c	20. d

TEST YOURSELF 12 (PAGE 85)

1.

Eb Major: III   bIII   biii   VI   bVI   bvi

2.

Bb Minor: iii   bIII   biii   vi   bVI   bvi

3.

A Major: III   bIII   biii   VI   bVI   bvi

4.

Ab Major: III   bIII   biii   VI   bVI   bvi

5.

E Minor: iii   #III   #iii   vi   #VI   #vi

TEST YOURSELF 13 (PAGE 97)

1. First chord:

    Db Major: Gr^6 (It would be spelled: B♭♭, D♭, F♭, G in this key.)
    D Major: V^7 (Correctly spelled in this key.)

    Second chord:
    D Major: $vii°^7$ (Correctly spelled in this key.)
    Db Major: $vii°^7/V$ (It would be spelled: G, B♭, D♭, F♭ in this key.)

2. C Major: $vii°^7/V$ (Correctly spelled in this key.)
    Eb Major: $vii°^7/V$ (It would be spelled: A, C, E♭, G♭ in this key.)

3. D Major: V^7 (Correctly spelled in this key.)
    Db Major: Gr^6 (It would be spelled: B♭♭, D♭, F♭, G in this key.)

4. Ab Major: $vii°^7$ (It would be spelled: G. B♭, D♭, F♭ in this key.)
    Cb Major: $vii°^7$ (Correctly spelled in this key.)

5. Ab Major: Gr^6 (It would be spelled; F♭, A♭, C♭, E in this key.)
    A Major: V^7 (Correctly spelled in this key.)

TEST YOURSELF 14 (PAGE 106)

1. It is quite chromatic (but there is some evidence of functional harmony).
2. The most common chord quality is the Mm7th chord (dominant 7th).

3. Chords 5–6 could be: **EM: ii V^7**.
   Chords 7–8 could be: **DM: Gr^6 V^7**.
   Chords 8–9 could be: **DM: V^7 I**.
   Chords 7–9 create a strong cadence in **D** Major.

4. Chords 1–4 are tied together by several chromatic relationships, most notably the chromatic sequence in the soprano: **F♯, G, G♯, A, B♭**.

5. On chords 2, 4, 7, and 9 there are accented nonharmonic tones in the soprano.
   a. Church modes
   b. Pentatonic scale   4 (upper part)
   c. Whole–tone scale   2
   d. 9th, 11th, and 13th chords   5
   e. Chords of addition and omission
   f. Quartal/quintal chords   1
   g. Linear cadence
   h. Third–relationship cadence   3 (enharmonic)
   i. Melodic doubling at various intervals   4
   j. Parallel chords (planing)   1,3

TEST YOURSELF 15 (PAGE 115)

a. Pandiatonicism   1
b. Polytonality   3,5
c. Dual modality
d. Shifted tonality
e. Free tonality
f. Polychords   1,2,4,5
g. Quartal/quintal chords 5
h. Clusters   2
i. Changing meter   5
j. Asymmetric meter
k. Nonaccentual rhythms   2

6.   7.   8.

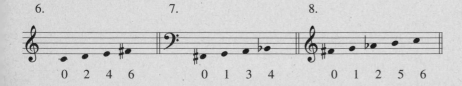

Dallapiccola: *Goethe-Lieder*, no. 2, for Mezzo-Soprano and E♭ Clarinet.

	I^0	I^1	I^{11}	I^9	I^3	I^8	I^6	I^7	I^2	I^5	I^4	I^{10}	
P^0	G#	A	G	F	B	E	D	D#	A#	C#	C	F#	R^0
P^{11}	G	G#	F#	E	A#	D#	C#	D	A	C	B	F	R^{11}
P^1	A	A#	G#	F#	C	F	D#	E	B	D	C#	G	R^1
P^3	B	C	A#	G#	D	G	F	F#	C#	E	D#	A	R^3
P^9	F	F#	E	D	G#	C#	B	C	G	A#	A	D#	R^9
P^4	C	C#	B	A	D#	G#	F#	G	D	F	E	A#	R^4
P^6	D	D#	C#	B	F	A#	G#	A	E	G	F#	C	R^6
P^5	C#	D	C	A#	E	A	G	G#	D#	F#	F	B	R^5
P^{10}	F#	G	F	D#	A	D	C	C#	G#	B	A#	E	R^{10}
P^7	D#	E	D	C	F#	B	A	A#	F	G#	G	C#	R^7
P^8	E	F	D#	C#	G	C	A#	B	F#	A	G#	D	R^8
P^2	A#	B	A	G	C#	F#	E	F	C	D#	D	G#	R^2
	RI^0	RI^1	RI^{11}	RI^9	RI^3	RI^8	RI^6	RI^7	RI^2	RI^5	RI^4	RI^{10}	

Dallapiccola: *Goethe-Lieder,* no. 2, for Mezzo-Soprano and E-flat Clarinet.

* *La parte del Clar. picc. è scritta in suoni reali.*

(The E-flat Clarinet part is written at sounding pitch.)